The Beginner's Handbook of Woodcarving

With Project Patterns for Line Carving,
Relief Carving, Carving in the Round, and Bird Carving

CHARLES BEIDERMAN AND
WILLIAM JOHNSTON

Dover Publications, Inc., *New York*

Bibliographical Note

This 1993 Dover edition is a slightly revised version of the one first published in 1988, which was an unabridged republication, with updated Appendix, of the work originally published by Prentice-Hall, Inc., Englewood Cliffs, New Jersey, in 1983.

Library of Congress Cataloging-in-Publication Data

Beiderman, Charles.
  The beginner's handbook of woodcarving.

  Reprint. Originally published: Englewood Cliffs, N.J. : Prentice-Hall, c1983.
  Bibliography: p.
  Includes index.
  1. Wood-carving.   I. Johnston, William, 1919–   II. Title.
[TT199.7.B44   1988]   736'.4   88-3686
ISBN-13: 978-0-486-25687-0
ISBN-10: 0-486-25687-1

Manufactured in the United States by Courier Corporation
25687116
www.doverpublications.com

Dedicated to our wives,
Margaret Beiderman and Lee Johnston,
for their patience, understanding, and encouragement;
and to the many warm friendships we have formed
through our years of woodcarving.

Contents

Preface

A woodcarver is one who can take a scrap of wood, breathe life into it with patient, skilled hands, and make it a warm object of lasting beauty. That is creativity.

This book, written with the beginner in mind, should enable the neophyte carver to enter the world of woodcarving and to develop the basic skills of the craft. Once you have set foot on this path, you will discover a certain kinship with the many others who have come before you, as well as those, both young and old, who appreciate the beauty of your craft. Wood has a warmth that cannot be duplicated in other mediums. It attains a soft patina and glow with the passage of time. Is it any wonder that antique wooden items are so sought after?

Throughout the ages, humans have always seemed to have a desire to express themselves through the carving of wood. The ancient Egyptians embellished their chariots with scenes of the hunt and victories in battle. The roving Norsemen carved fearsome dragon heads on the prows of the longships. Spanish galleons were adorned with ornate carvings. His Britannic Majesty's ships of the line under the command of Lord Nelson were not without their carved fancywork. Indeed, Yankee clippers were graced with figureheads that were the product of the carver's art.

The famed churches of Europe and England are veritable museums of the woodcarver's skill, admired by thousands to this day. Every land has its artisans in carving. Our own American Indians carved decoy ducks in order to lure waterfowl within range of their bows; the Indians of the Northwest carved majestic totem poles and war canoes from logs; and a trip to the Southwest will take you to the Navahos and their carved Kachina dolls. The natives of Africa carved their version of the animals of the jungle. In the Caribbean and in South America primitive carvings in mahogany abound. To the natives of New Guinea carved masks are an important part of their culture. The Maoris of New Zealand carved images of their gods; and even Australian aborigines carved crude designs on their boomerangs.

In lands where wood was scarce or nonexistent, people always found the means to carve. The Eskimo carved walrus tusks, bone, and soft stones; the Chinese, jade and semiprecious stones; and the people of India and the Far East carved intricate designs in ivory and teak.

So you see, your wish to take a tool in hand and express yourself is not new; it is a deep-seated desire felt by all peoples down through history.

In this book you will be introduced to the various carving tools and their uses, as well as the advantages and disadvantages of many different kinds of wood. The various forms of woodcarving—line carving, relief carving, and carving in the round—are all described, and a series of patterns is supplied for each category, with a special chapter devoted to bird carving.

It has become quite obvious to us from reading various craft publications and talking with other carvers that there is a growing demand among the ever-expanding list of new carvers for a source of patterns from which to carve interesting pieces. Therefore, this book is also designed to help fill the void in needed patterns and to provide a wider spectrum of ideas for both the beginner and the advanced carver. Many carvers have improved their skill in the process of creating several fine pieces only to find that they have exhausted their ideas. Many carvers are fine craftspeople, but they lack the artistic ability to draw or create patterns. Our desire to answer these needs has resulted in the writing of this book.

The patterns shown in this book are not solely the work of the authors; they are a collection of designs graciously offered by our many carving friends. In attempting to provide a cross section of patterns for the different forms of carving, we have included a variety of subjects—humorous characters, birds, animals, flowers, and so on—to meet the needs of as many carvers as possible. However, no one book could ever contain enough ideas to satisfy the interests of all carvers. We feel it is sufficient if the patterns found here provide readers with the inspiration to go ahead and create something of special significance to themselves.

Although one would think that different carvers working from a particular pattern would produce identical pieces, this is seldom so. Each carver views the subject in a different light and with a different interpretation. The plan simply serves as a basic concept. For example, one might carve a robin with the head in a straight-forward position; another will vary this by cutting off the head, twisting it, and regluing it into a position that has the bird looking off in another direction. Still another carver will change the position of the legs and feet. One might see a humorous character as tall and slender, while another might wish it more robust. Facial expressions will also vary in the hands of the carver.

Throughout the book we give pointers on carving particular pieces to get you over the difficult stages. Tips on painting and finishing your work are also included. We were unable to include specific coloring instructions for all of the pieces. Unfortunately, the cost of research is high. However, there are other good books and aids that provide this information, and they are available from your local library or book shop.

How to go about exhibiting and entering your carvings in competition is outlined here for the first time in any book of woodcarving. You will be told how to form a carving club and all the advantages that can be gained from such an organization, another subject never before discussed in books on carving. Finally, you will learn how to apply your skill to many gifts for your friends and how to create an art form that can be offered for sale.

We hope you will find this book enjoyable!

Acknowledgments

We wish to extend our deep appreciation to the following persons and organizations for their help in preparing the contents of this book. Without their willingness to help, it would have been impossible.

Artwork. Timothy Cahill (line drawing of patterns), William Goudy (bird patterns).

Photography. Martin Basmajian, Karl Gramlich, William Rigney, Kronschnabel Studios of Cornwells Heights, PA.

Pattern Ideas. Martin Hesch, Thomas Koons, Eldred W. Atkinson, L. E. Trimble. Figures 7-1b, 7-2b, 7-3, 7-4, 7-5, 7-6, and 7-7 are reprinted with permission from the National Wildlife Federation.

Research materials. Philadelphia Academy of Natural

Science (mounted bird specimens); Clifford Huston (carving screw) 2533 Reese St., Philadelphia, PA 19148; Glass House Catalogue, Van Dyke Supply Company, Woonsocket, SD (for allowing us to adapt their bird eye sizes); Elmer Jumper (carver's benches) 142 Di'Marco Dr., Philadelphia, PA 19154; Pennsylvania Game Commission (bird and animal charts); and the private and governmental agencies (charts and pictorial material).

Carvings. Julius Hayden (carvings of four stages of carving a figure in the round).

And finally, thanks to all our friends, from whom we have learned many things and to whom we will be eternally grateful. We would also extend a special thank-you to the many members of the Pennsylvania Delaware Valley Woodcarvers, who encouraged us as beginners in the craft of woodcarving.

1

Getting started

The fact that you have picked up this book indicates your interest in woodcarving. Who knows what sparked this interest? Perhaps you have read a newspaper or magazine article about a carver, or maybe you have seen a display of carvings that caught your fancy. Perhaps you attended a woodcarving show and the desire to try your hand at woodcarving was born. No matter, the important thing is you want to carve!

Your first efforts will be crude, but that is to be expected, so don't be discouraged. Remember, the most skillful of carvers had to start out just like you. They, too, experienced the day when they made their first cut into wood. With patience, your skill will improve with each carving. Start with a simple project, learn how to work with the grain of the wood, get the feel of your tools, and you will be well on your way.

A professional carver tells of his apprenticeship in Germany. For the first three months he wasn't allowed to touch a piece of wood but had to devote himself to the care and sharpening of tools. The following three months were spent in making practice cuts in scrap wood to get the feel of the tools that are so much a part of woodcarving. We don't expect you to follow such a rigid regimen, but mention it only to stress the importance of the elementary steps—one must crawl before one can walk.

Of course, we are not discussing woodcarving on a professsional level but rather as a hobby that will bring forth a lifetime of pleasure. There is no better way to relax after the rigors of the working day than to sit at your workbench with a carving in hand. With each cut of the knife the cares and worries of the world seem to lift from your shoulders. Soon you will find you are whistling or humming a tune as the chips fall from your workbench.

Carving is a craft of inspiration and talking to other carvers, so the things to do to get started are subscribe to a woodcarving publication and join a club. One of the first things you should do is join the National Wood Carvers Association. This organization, started in the early 1950s with just a handful of members, has grown to a membership of many thousands. (Write to National Wood Carvers Association, 7424 Miami Avenue, Cincinnati, Ohio 45243, for the location of chapters in your area.)

The primary benefit of membership in this informally organized association is that every two months you will receive *Chip Chats,* a journal offering information on recent carving techniques and tools, patterns, articles on carving, reviews of carving shows, and a calendar of events of interest to carvers. The annual March/April issue lists a comprehensive review of sources of carving-related items such as wood, tools, books, carving kits, patterns, carving schools, and possible sales outlets for your completed carvings. This issue alone is worth the cost of membership. At present the N.W.C.A. has no provisions governing the establishment and functioning of local clubs. Each carving club is an independent unit free to govern itself.

If you live on the West Coast, you may want to consider a membership in the California Carvers Guild (P.O. Box 1195, Cambria, California 93428), another very fine organization with much to offer; its publication is entitled *The CCG Log.*

Another fine publication, well worth the price of subscription, is *The Mallet,* published monthly by The National Carvers Museum, 14960 Woodcarvers Road, Monument, Colorado 80132. This magazine also offers similar information and both are excellent means of communication and a sharing of knowledge from carvers throughout the world.

Becoming a member of a carving club will bring you many advantages, the most important of which will be the sharing of knowledge. You will be able to talk with other carvers whom otherwise you would not have the opportunity to meet. The kinds of problems you run into can be discussed and solved. (Specific procedures for forming your own carving club are discussed in Chapter 11.)

An active woodcarving club offers much to its members. The authors have been affiliated with the Pennyslvania

Delaware Valley Wood Carvers for many years, and it provides an excellent example. Organized to further the warm fellowship, interests, and skills of woodcarvers and whittlers, the club serves the beginner as well as the advanced carver. It meets once a month, and its programs include a show-and-tell period at each meeting, in which members bring in a carving and discuss it. The following activities are offered: spring and fall courses for both the beginner and the more advanced carver, an annual wood auction, a library of woodcarving books, and field trips to places of interest to carvers.

The club sets up a monthly display of members' carvings in banks, libraries, and schools. Members also give talks and demonstrations to schoolchildren and Scout troops on the subject of woodcarving. The resource chairman maintains a file that helps members obtain information on where to purchase tools, wood, patterns, books, and other carving-related items. Free lessons are offered in the care and sharpening of tools. Meetings often include instruction periods in tool technique, the use of the burning pen, the fine points of face carving, the making of birds' feet, and the painting of birds. An informative newsletter is published monthly, and, of course, the highlight of the year is the annual woodcarvers' show, in which each member is encouraged to exhibit his or her work.

As a measure of its success, this club, which started with just 5 people interested in working with wood, has grown to a membership of over 175 men and women from all walks of life. We may be clerks, tradespeople, truck drivers, sales representatives, clergy, executives, retired folk, or workers in the home, but when we come through the door of our meeting room, we are just one thing—woodcarvers!

2
Wood:
the living medium

Various carving woods

If there were only one piece of advice we could give you, it would be, Don't stint on wood. Remember, you are going to invest a goodly number of hours in your carving, so even if you must spend a few dollars more, begin with a good piece of wood. We learned this lesson with one of our first attempts at figure carving. A piece of scrap fir was used, and things seemed to go fairly well until it was time to carve the facial details, which had been saved until last. The wide grain of the fir just wouldn't support fine carving, so the many hours put into the carving were wasted. Had basswood or sugar pine been used, that little figure would be sitting on the living room bookshelf today.

Most woods can be carved, but some are much better than others. Willow, yew, and Phillippine mahogany (Luan), for example, tend to be stringy, and redwood and some cedars are prone to splitting. Most of the woods found at local lumberyards are fine for building projects but leave too much to be desired when it comes to woodcarving. Balsa wood is great for model gliders, but for woodcarving . . . forget it!

On the other hand, basswood, American cousin to European linden, is excellent as a carving wood. White pine and sugar pine also have fine carving properties. These woods are close-grained and will permit the fine carving of detailwork. They do not possess the beautiful grains found in the harder woods, but if you are going to paint your carving, basswood or sugar pine would be your best bet.

5

If your carving is to have a natural finish, walnut is a top carving wood with a warm, appealing grain, as are apple, cherry, plum, and any of the fruitwoods. Honduras mahogany is close-grained with a reddish hue; oak and elm have their own pleasing grain characteristics; butternut, as its name denotes, is a light-colored wood with excellent carving qualities; and we are all familiar with the red and white grain of cedar. Poplar is also an easily carved wood but often has a greenish cast throughout the grain.

One word of caution: Some of the exotic woods, such as rosewood and cocobolo contain toxic substances that could result in skin rashes and respiratory problems. In working with these woods it is advisable to wear long sleeves and to use a dust mask as a precautionary measure.

The following chart lists the more readily available woods. In addition, there are many imported exotic woods that can be purchased from wood specialty houses. Some fine carving woods may be native to your section of the country—try them!

WOOD REFERENCE CHART

Wood	Grain	Color	Comments
Basswood	Close	Light creamy	Excellent carving wood, especially for detailwork. Does not have attractive grain pattern.
Beech	Close	White with reddish tint	Fine for carving bowls, utensils; no odor or taste. Prone to checking.
Birch	Close	Creamy	Works well. Sturdy wood. Attractive grain patterns.
Butternut	Moderate	Butter color	Good carving wood but prone to chipping.
Cedar	Close	White with red or purple streaks	Good carving if you work around knots. Pleasing odor, beautiful grain. A good exterior wood.
Chestnut	Moderate to coarse	Reddish brown	Easy carving, nice texture. Tends to be wormy. Prone to checking.
Cypress	Close to wide	Reddish brown	Easy carving. Holds up to weather.
Elm	Close to moderate	Light brown	A medium-hard wood. Takes a good finish.
Fruitwoods Apple	Moderate	Tan, creamy	Easy carving with interesting grain patterns. Takes beautiful natural finish. Tends to be wormy.

Cherry	Close	Reddish tan	Good carving wood. Beautiful grain, takes nice natural finish.
Pear	Moderate	Creamy	Good carving wood. Will support detail carving.
Plum	Close	Light purple	Good carving wood. Interesting grain colorations.
Holly	Very close	White	Difficult to obtain. Excellent for fine detail. Pure white when carved but gradually darkens with age.
Honduras mahogany	Open, moderate	Reddish brown	Excellent carving wood. Pleasing natural finish.
Magnolia	Close	Pale green, brown, and yellow	Good carving, Interesting color grain. Finishes well.
Maple	Moderate	Creamy	Medium hard to carve.
Oak	Coarse	Tan to brown	Not too good for fine detail but a good carving wood. Has great strength.
Philippine mahogany (Luan)	Stringy	Reddish brown	Grain often wild; not straight. Often difficult to carve. Takes a nice natural finish.
Pine, white	Close	White	Excellent carving wood. Now becoming scarce.
Pine, sugar	Close	Creamy, tan	Good carving wood for painted carvings. Resin flecks must be well sealed. Can be detail-carved. Does not have attractive grain.
Poplar	Close	White with some light-green streaks.	Easy to carve but not particularly strong. Interesting grain coloration.
Redwood	Medium	Dark reddish brown	Cuts easily but quite limited for detail carving. Tends to split and splinter. Good for exterior use.
Walnut	Close	Chocolate brown to purple	The king of carving woods. So excellent, many professional carvers will use nothing else. Beautiful grain patterns. Takes superb natural finish.

Inexpensive ways to obtain wood for carving

Wood is all around us, and much of it is excellent for carving. Old barn timbers were often made of white pine or chestnut. A barn or house that is in the process of being demolished will yield untold quantities of good seasoned wood. (Just make a careful check for nails or the sharp edges of your tools will suffer.)

Many of the old-timers down in the Chesapeake Bay area carve their famed decoys from discarded telephone poles. Old cedar lantern posts and wooden rain gutters that have been replaced with modern-day aluminum can be made into objects of beauty for years to come. If there are boat-building or cabinetmaking shops in your area, you can usually have cutoffs and scraps of mahogany for the taking. And most sawmills will let you have slabs of bark for mounting your carved birds at no cost.

Once it is known to your friends that you are a wood-carver, you will have many offers of wood. For instance, when someone is about to have a fruit tree cut down, he or she will probably be glad to let you take your pick of the wood. Recently a neighbor cut down a holly tree that had grown too large for a foundation planting and presented us with the trunk. Holly, being a close-grain wood, is much prized for its fine carving quality. When freshly cut, it is pure white and, much like old ivory, mellows to a cream color with the passing of years.

You will find yourself collecting all sorts of interesting pieces of wood for mounts. Roots of bushes and trees and gnarled branches make excellent mountings for birds. Sections of old grapevines are perfect for this purpose, and driftwood is just the thing for carved waterfowl and gulls. You won't find much driftwood along ocean beaches, though, the shores of bays, lakes, rivers, and streams are the places to look. Take along a small pruning saw when you go on your driftwood safari; many times a piece too large to bring home will have some interesting-looking branches.

Old furniture will often provide wood for carving. Beautiful plaques have been carved from the leaves and tops of old mahogany tables and chests that have been bought for a few dollars at sales and auctions. Crating wood, especially from items that have been imported, may—when planed, sanded, and stained—reveal hidden beauty. Tongue depressors, available from your druggist, are usually made of birch and carve well. They are useful for tail feathers for small birds that require wood stronger than sugar pine or basswood. Slats from a discarded basswood Venetian blind can also be utilized in a similar manner.

Many carving clubs hold annual wood auctions where members donate their surplus wood to be auctioned off for the benefit of the club treasury. Often choice pieces of wood can be picked up at a fraction of their commerical prices in this manner.

Finally, if you have a particular project in mind, such as the carving of a family crest or coat of arms, that calls for a specific kind or thickness of wood, don't hesitate to purchase wood from a wood specialty house. (Several good outlets are listed in the appendix of this book. In addition, each year the March April issue of *Chip Chats* lists about fifteen pages of suppliers of wood, books, and carving-related items; other carving magazines carry similar advertisements.)You will never regret your investment of time or money if it results in an object of beauty of which you can be proud.

How to season wood

Although it is possible to carve green wood, your chances of success will be much greater if you use cured wood. Due to the fact that the heartwood (core) dries at a different rate from the sapwood (outer wood), stresses and strains take place as the green wood dries out. These stresses cause logs to split and the ends to check (crack from the center of the log to the bark).

Air-drying is therefore advised in order to slow the drying process down to a more even rate. This is accomplished by painting or waxing the cut ends and openings in the bark wherever side branches have been lopped off. A good method is to take an old candle and coat the exposed wood with melted wax. With a pencil, mark the date you are starting the seasoning process.

The wood should then be stored in a dry, airy place, away from sun and rain, with pieces of scrap wood positioned between the logs or timber to promote air circulation. Every six months turn the wood, inspecting the ends to see if checking has opened the sealant; if it has, apply more wax. After eighteen months your wood should have cured and will be ready for carving.

Some carvers claim that logs season better if they are stripped of their bark. If you are seasoning your logs in your garage or dry cellar, this might be advantageous, because the bark usually plays host to many undesirable insects.

You will find home-curing more successful if you first trim out the green log into beams and planks, since logs are more susceptible to checking and splitting and also take longer to cure. Again, liberally coat the ends of each piece with a sealant.

Most commercial woods are kiln-dried, a process whereby timber is placed in large ovens and dried slowly with controlled heat. Smaller pieces of wood may be cured chemically by immersion in PEG 1000 for twenty-four hours, which prevents checking and shrinkage. This water-soluble wood stabilizer is available from Craftsman Wood Service Co., 1735 West Cortland Court, Addison, Illinois 60101; Constantines, 2050 Eastchester Road, Bronx, New York 10461; or H. E. Wheeler, 2230 E 49th Street, Tulsa, Oklahoma 74105. This process, however, cannot be used on woods you wish to stain, because the wood cells are sealed in such a manner as to prevent absorption of stains and penetrating finishes.

If you do wish to work with green wood, the secret of carving it is to drill a hole completely through it from top to bottom. This allows for expansion and contraction of the wood as it dries out. Once drying has occurred, you can fit a wood plug into the uppermost hole and carve it to conform with the design. European carvers have often carved masks and plaques of green wood, hollowing out the reverse side to prevent cracks and splitting.

3
Tools for carving

One of the great things about wood carving is that you don't have to buy expensive equipment to get started. Unlike in photography, boating, restoring antique cars, and so on, a few basic tools and a block of wood can see you off to a good start. Of course, as you progress, you may wish to add to your basic tools, primarily because of timesaving factors. For centuries craftspeople and artisans have created works of art with just the simplest of hand tools, so don't feel you cannot create credible work unless you have a workshop full of sophisticated power tools. Andy Anderson, famed carver of Western caricatures, whose whittled cowpokes are today much-sought-after collector's items, used little more than a homemade knife ground down from an old straight razor. So you see, it is the skill in the heart and in the hands that counts, not the expensive tool.

In addition to the basic household tools found in every home, there are a few simple tools that will fill a beginner's requirements. We recommend that you try to have on hand the following:

Several carving knives

Sharpening stones, light oil

Leather strop

Surform half-round and round rasps

Coping saw with a variety of blades

Vise

C clamps (6-inch or more)

Workbench with good light

Drill and assorted bits

Glue (Titebond, Elmer's)

Epoxy putty

No-load aluminum oxide sandpaper (coarse, medium, and fine)

Acrylic paints, brushes

As your carving skills improve, you will probably want to pick up additional tools to fill specific needs. This can be done gradually over a period of years, so that a huge initial cash outlay is not required. We purposely did not include chisels, firmers, and gouges in the list of basic tools. Try several projects using just your knives so that you can get the feel of a wood-cutting tool and the characteristics of various kinds of wood. After you have gained this experience, buy other edged tools as you find it necessary.

Don't make the mistake of rushing out and buying a complete set of carving tools. "Quality instead of quantity" should be your watchword. Often a well-meaning wife will buy her husband an expensive set of tools for Christmas or his birthday only to find that just a few will actually be used. Perhaps the best path to follow would be to sign up for a carving course and buy only the few tools your instructor recommends.

Bear in mind that all edged tools are sold with a "store edge" (in other words, unsharpened). They will all have to be sharpened, honed, and stropped before use in carving.

It is generally conceded that the best carving tools come from England, Germany, and Switzerland. The criterion of a good tool is how well it will hold an edge. Look for a blade of carbon steel for best results.

Now let us take a closer look at the tools you will be using. Many excellent tools can be made by you at home, and we shall give instructions on how to accomplish this in the pages that follow.

Knives

When one thinks of a person working with wood with a knife, there comes to mind the image of an old-timer sitting on the front porch of the general store with his chair tilted back, whittling away with his trusty pocket knife. This is all well and good, and every person worth his or her salt should carry a good pocket knife. However, when it comes to carving, *a knife with a fixed blade is preferable*. Despite caution, a folding blade can close at the wrong time and inflict a painful cut. Furthermore, better control can be obtained with a knife with a short, rigid blade that is solidly and permanently set into a comfortable handle.

Knives come in a variety of shapes and types. Certain companies, such as X-acto, Stanley, and the Warren Company, offer a knife with interchangeable blades. The knives

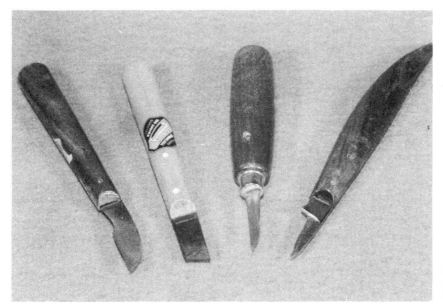

Figure 3-1a Good carving knives with short, rigid blades and comfortable handles.

Figure 3-1b Set of knives with interchangeable blades. *Photo courtesy of Warren Tools, Route 1, Box 12B, Rhinebeck, N.Y. 12575.*

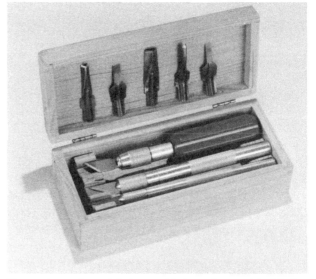

Figure 3-1c Set of knives with interchangeable blades and chisels. *Photo courtesy of P.O. Instrument Co., 13 Lehigh Ave, Paterson, N.J. 07503.*

of the Warren Company of Rhinebeck, New York, are exceptionally fine, the blades being custom-ground of fine Swedish tungsten steel and the handle made with a solid brass jaw. Single-blade knives from Germany and Switzerland are available from tool specialty houses. You will, no doubt, end up with a variety of knives. Just keep in mind that any knife not kept sharp is of little use.

When working with a knife, strive to use the muscle power of your fingers and hand rather than that of your arm.

Don't use the kind of stroke you'd use for sharpening a pencil; this utilizes strong muscle power from the arm but furnishes very little control. Instead, make it a practice to use some of the basic knife cuts as shown.

Types of knife cuts

The one basic rule is always to cut with the grain. For example, if you are carving a round area, such as a bird's eye or the letter Q, think of the area to be carved as a clockface with the grain of the wood running from 12 o'clock to 6 o'clock. Carve with your sharp knife from the 12 o'clock to the 3 o'clock position, then from the 6 o'clock to the 3 o'clock point. On the other side of the circle, carve from 12 o'clock to 9 o'clock, then up from 6 o'clock to 9 o'clock. (See Figure 3-2A.)

The paring cut

A cut with excellent control, useful in carving fine detail. Grasp the knife as you would if you were paring an apple. The thumb is braced against the wood, while the sharp blade is drawn toward the thumb by the pressure formed by the closing motion of the fingers. This makes for short, very accurate cuts.

The slicing cut

A cut made with the point of the knife inserted with the edge at a 45-degree (or less) angle and drawn the length of the desired cut. For firmer control, the index finger may be placed on the back of the blade, with the heel of the hand resting on the wood for support. The slicing cut can also be used as a stop cut. This cut is especially useful in outlining the subject in line and relief carving. It is used in carving fine detail such as facial features and fingers.

The thumb-push cut

Many times when you are carving a tight spot, it will be impossible to use the paring cut. If your work is clamped down or held in a vise, the thumb from your other hand may be used to exert pressure on the back of the knife blade.

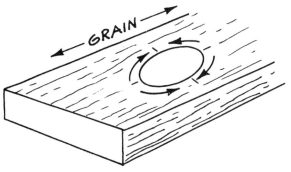

Figure 3-2a Cutting an arc.

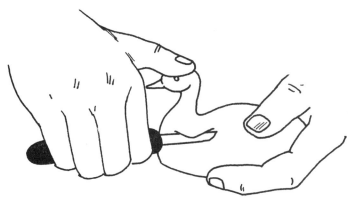

Figure 3-2b Paring cut.

Figure 3-2c William Johnston illustrating the paring cut.

Figure 3-2d Slicing cut.

Figure 3-2f Rocking cut.

Figure 3-2e Thumb-push cut.

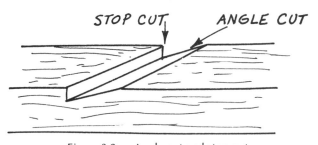

STOP CUT   ANGLE CUT

Figure 3-2g Angle cut and stop cut.

The rocking cut

Often used in chip carving. The point of the knife is inserted in the wood, and the blade is rocked down. This is a forceful cut and is often needed for cutting across the grain.

The stop cut

Used extensively in relief and incise carving. A vertical cut is made into the wood to act as a stop. The next cut (angle cut) is directed into the stop cut, which prevents the removal of wood from the uncut area on the other side of the stop cut.

The angle cut

The angle cut is a cut made with the side of the blade at an angle to the wood surface. Used in conjunction with the stop cut, it can make for controlled removal of unwanted wood. Bear in mind that the unwanted wood should be cleanly cut free; avoid breaking the wood loose.

Chisels

You will find chisels, when used correctly, indispensable in fast removal of large quantities of wood. They are available in standard, miniature, and subminiature sizes and will enable you to get results not obtainable with carving knives, for example, the recessed background of a relief carving. Most European-trained carvers use chisels exclusively, even carving facial features and hair with them.

For the wood-carver the term *chisel* actually covers a variety of categories, each with its own purpose.

The following tools come with both straight and bent shafts in widths from 1 millimeter to 35 millimeters. They also come in a great variety of edges, from shallow to deep shaped. Consult a good tool catalog for the sizes and shapes you may wish to purchase.

Carpenter's or flat chisel

Sharpened on one side only, it has a flat-surfaced cutting edge. Used for roughing out. Care must be taken to prevent digging in.

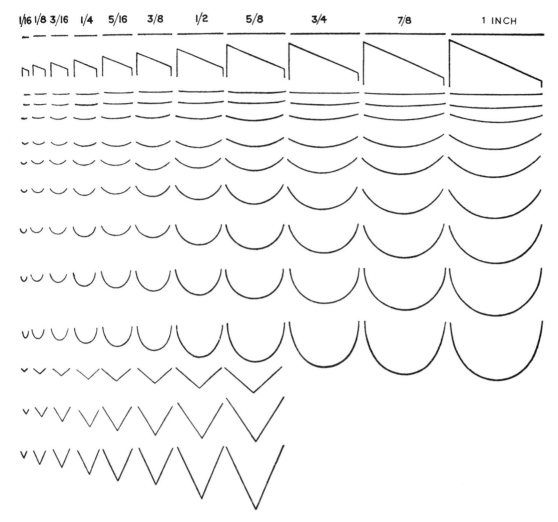

1/16	1/8	3/16	1/4	5/16	3/8	1/2	5/8	3/4	7/8	1 INCH

Figure 3-3   Sizes and sweeps (cutting edges) of woodcarving tools.
This chart is reprinted by permission of Taylor Tool Company.

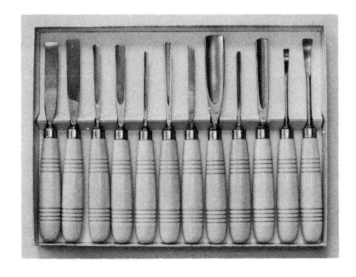

Figure 3-4   Set of chisels.
*Courtesy of Pentalic
Corp., 132 W. 22nd St.,
New York, N. Y. 10011.*

Firmer

A chisel sharpened on both sides, which are slightly rounded toward the tip. This tool will not have the tendency to "dig in" as will the flat chisel and is often used to smooth a carved wood surface.

Skew

A chisel whose cutting edge is at an angle; very useful for undercutting or cleaning out corners.

Veiner or fluter

A chisel with a *U*-shaped blade; useful for hollowing out a surface, grooving, and outlining.

Gouge

A chisel with a curved cutting edge. It makes a semicircular cut in wood. Used for the same purpose as the veiner where a more shallow cut is desired.

Parting or V tool

A chisel with a *V*-shaped cutting edge. Used for undercutting, finishing inside corners, and outlining. On animal carvings, it is often used to carve hair or fur.

With grinding and honing, old files can be made into flat chisels and skews. A complete set of miniature chisels for finework can be made at practically no cost out of flat-cut hard-steel 8D nails. Drill a hole in a section of an old broomstick for a handle. Apply epoxy glue, and drive the nail into the hole. Once it is set, use a power grinder to shape the nail head into a cutting edge, taking care to dip the nail in water frequently to keep it cool. Whetting, honing, and stropping will provide you with a small tool with a keen edge. Of course, frequent touching up on a stone will be necessary while carving, but you will have a miniature tool that can get into those wee nooks and crannies.

Many knives for specific purposes can be made with a little ingenuity and patience. An excellent carving knife can be made by grinding down a straight-edged razor and fitting it with a handle. Knife blades can also be fashioned from old hacksaw blades.

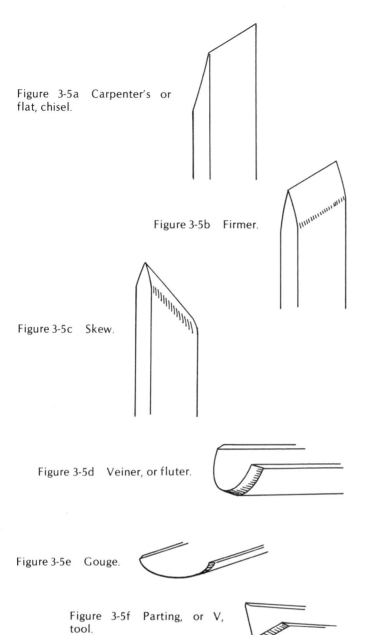

Figure 3-5a Carpenter's or flat, chisel.

Figure 3-5b Firmer.

Figure 3-5c Skew.

Figure 3-5d Veiner, or fluter.

Figure 3-5e Gouge.

Figure 3-5f Parting, or V, tool.

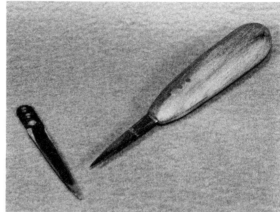

Figure 3-6a Homemade knife and chisel.

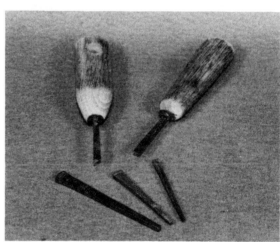

Figure 3-6b Chisels made from common cut nails.

Sharpening stones
and how to use them

Sharpening stones come in a variety of types and shapes. The best natural stone is considered to be the soft Washita for fast cutting. Many man-made stones come with a medium grit on one side and a fine grit on the other. A hard Arkansas stone is used to finish off, after which the edge should be stropped.

Use a honing oil or a light oil as a lubricant when using the stone. The purpose of this is to float away the micro-

Figure 3-7   Sharpening stones and oil.

scopic pieces of steel and to prevent them from clogging the grit of your stone. Periodically clean your stone by scrubbing it with kerosene and an old toothbrush. Some carvers heat the stone in the oven to "bake" out the saturated oil and dirt. Make it a practice to wipe off your stone after each use and place it in a dustproof container.

If your blade is nicked, it will have to be ground on a grindstone. Use a light touch, wetting the blade frequently to prevent overheating and drawing out the temper.

When using a whetstone to sharpen a knife, apply honing oil or very light oil to the stone, then place the blade flat on the stone. Raise the back of the blade about 15 degrees, and push the edge the length of the stone. After 6 or 8 strokes, reverse the blade and repeat with the same number of strokes on the other side. Continue until a sharp edge results. The knife is then ready for honing on a hard Arkansas stone.

The finishing touch is applied by stropping on a leather strop. Many carvers favor rubbing jeweler's rouge or buffing compound into the leather strop as a fine abrasive.

Flat chisels are sharpened in a similar manner, except that only the angle side of the blade is worked on the stone.

A skew chisel is sharpened on both sides like a knife blade.

The V tool is sharpened as if it were two flat chisels, working each edged surface of the V in turn.

Due to their concave cutting edges, a little more care must be exercised when sharpening gouges. Most gouges have a ground bevel of about 15 degrees. Applying a few drops of honing oil or light lubricating oil onto a fine-textured oilstone, hold the gouge at right angles to it at the 15-degree bevel. As you draw it along the full length of the stone, simultaneously twist the gouge with a wrist motion so that the entire surface of the bevel comes into contact with the stone (Figure 3-8A). Avoid overtwisting, as this will result in rounded corners, which is not desirable. Continue honing until a sharp edge results.

The inner surface of the cutting edge is then honed with an oilstone slip. The slipstone is wedge shaped, with two rounded edges to accommodate gouges of various curvatures. After applying oil, the slipstone is held at the same 15-degree angle and rubbed back and forth on the inside curvature of the edge (Figure 3-8B). The gouge is then ready to be stropped to remove the wire edge. A piece of soft leather treated with crocus powder and light oil is used. Using the same method as in honing, strop the gouge on the soft leather, which has first been placed on a flat surface (Figure 3-8C).

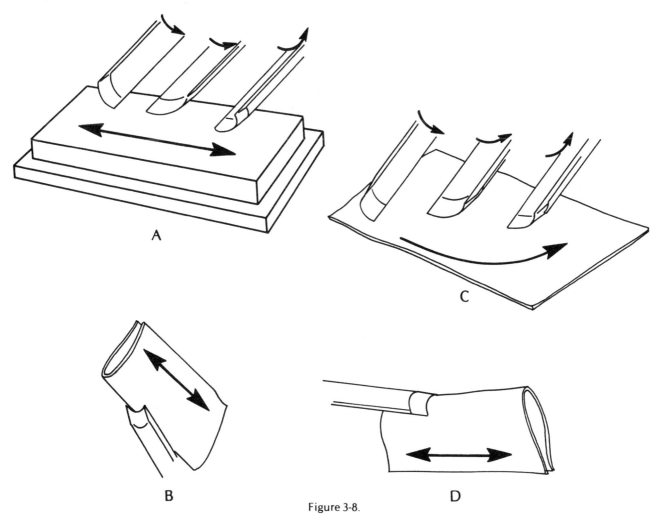

A

C

B

D

Figure 3-8.

To strop the inside bevel, fold the leather to conform with the inside curvature and draw it in strokes away from the handle of the gouge (Figure 3-8D).

Always remember when using a stone that the edge of the tool is pushed toward the stone. The exception is in the use of gouges, which are rolled sideways. When using the strop, the edge is drawn away against the leather. Make it a habit when carving to touch up your edged tools often on your stone and strop.

Make blade guards for your knives and chisels from folded cardboard and glass filament tape. The few moments taken to make them will reward you with the protection it will afford those sharp edges when the tools are not in use.

The poor-man's sharpening system

An inexpensive tool-sharpening system can be made from common materials. The most important material needed to complete your system will be a final buffing compound obtained from a material that is discarded by your local bowling alley. Make a visit to a nearby bowling alley and ask them for the worn-out wheels from the ball-polishing machine. This is composed of a very fine buffing compound. Break the stone into convenient pieces for better handling. The wheel can be sawn into handy pieces with a band saw, but you should know that the abrasive action of the material will destroy the cutting edge of the saw blade. This should, therefore, be done with an old blade that you do not care to

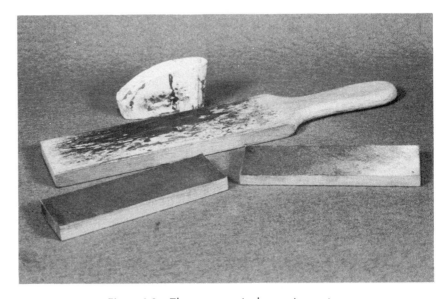

Figure 3-9   The poor-man's sharpening system.

keep. You will also need a sheet each of the following grades of very fine no-load sandpaper: Carborundum 180 Silicone Carbide and Norton No-Fill Durite 150A.

The system is composed of three units made in the following manner: Glue the sandpaper to a convenient-sized block of wood. Shape a stropping stick similar to that shown. For the actual tool sharpening, first carefully strop the knife or tool over the 180 paper and remove any nicks from the edge. Then strop the edge on the 150A paper to make a finer cut. Finally take the strop stick and scrub a liberal coating of the buffing material from the bowling-ball-polishing machine over the surface of the stick. Take your knife or tool in hand and strop it across the surface, reversing the blade with each stroke. You will thus have put a keen edge on your tool.

As you carve, from time to time you will want to restore that fine edge on your knife quickly and without going to a lot of trouble. A touch-up stick on your workbench will enable you to do just that. Cut a 16-inch-long square piece of wood that measures 2 inches on each side. At one end drill a hole that will later hold a leather thong for hanging. On this same end whittle a comfortable handle. Cut a piece of rubber from an old inner tube or some sponge rubber to act as a pad. Tack down one end, stretch it until taut, then tack down the remaining end. Over this rubber pad tack a strip of 180-grit no-load aluminum oxide abrasive cloth. Now turn your stick over, and to the reverse side cement a length of untreated leather, which you will use for final stropping. On one of the remaining sides rub buffing compound when you are ready to touch up your blade. Strop your knife on the abrasive-cloth side, then stroke it a dozen times on the buffing compound, and finish with a stropping on the leather surface. All this takes but a minute, and you will be rewarded by being able to carve with a keen edge.

Mallets

When you progress to where you will be using chisels and gouges, you will need a mallet. By all means, choose a carver's mallet as shown in Figure 3-10. Don't use a hammer, unless you want to reduce your tool handles to splinters. If you have access to a wood-turning lathe, you can turn out a fine mallet from seasoned hardwood that will serve for many years. We know carvers who made dandy mallets out of an old baseball bat and old bowling pins (Figures 3-11A-B).

Figure 3-10   The carver's mallet.

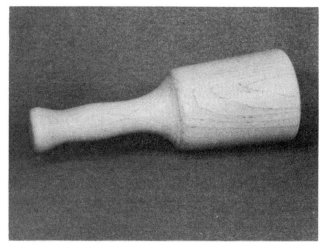

Figure 3-11   A handy mallet can be turned from an old bowling pin.

Bottoming-out router

When doing certain relief carving, you will find it difficult to level the bottom surface in the background area accurately. This simple device will do the job quite well. It is constructed of scrap wood and an inexpensive offset screwdriver that has been sharpened in such a manner as to produce a scraping sharp angle, which acts as a chisel as it moves across the surface of the carving.

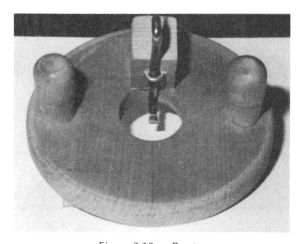

Figure 3-12a   Router.

Figure 3-12b   Router in use.

Rasps

You will find the Surform half-round and round rasps indispensable for the quick removal of wood. After you have cut the top and side views of your carving in the round, the Surform rasp will make quick work of rounding off those

24

Figure 3-13   Metal sanding rasps.

corners and getting your squared block down to the point where you are ready to do the actual carving. These handy tools have replaceable blades and can be obtained in the hardware section of any good department store or your local hardware dealer.

A very useful set of handy metal sanding rasps can be made from strips of punched hardened metal sanding mesh, such as that manufactured by Red Devil (Figure 3-13). By cutting the metal with a pair of scissors or snips and carefully bending it around a square or round form, such as dowel sticks of various sizes, a complete set can be made. These are useful in concave areas, such as the neck of a bird or a duck. For use on a convex or flat surface, the material can be affixed to a flat block or tongue depressor. To fasten the metal to the wooden form, it is recommended that the same kind of contact cement be used as the type that is used to bond laminated surfaces to countertops. Use the cement sparingly to prevent clogging the holes in the metal. Coat each piece separately and allow it to dry to the touch, then bring the pieces together in a tight bond.

Bow sander

A very convenient and useful tool for sanding hard-to-reach places can easily be fashioned from a piece of plywood with clamping devices held by wing nuts at each end. Cut narrow strips of emery cloth into lengths and secure them in a taut manner under the end clamps. To save time in changing emery strips, you may wish to make three bow sanders; one each for coarse, medium, and fine emery.

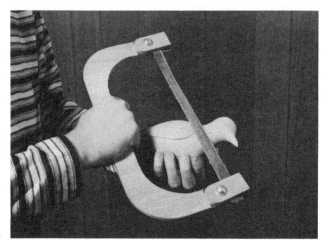

Figure 3-14   The bow sander.

Pyroelectric or burning pen

The burning pen has many uses in woodcarving. Greater realism may be attained through the careful use of this tool, especially in the feather-texturing of birds and waterfowl. The shaggy effect of miniature dogs, bear, buffalo, and so forth can be gained with a burning pen as well as with a carving tool.

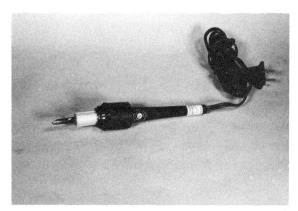
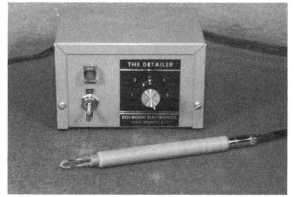

Figure 3-15a & b   The pyrolectic, or burning, pen.

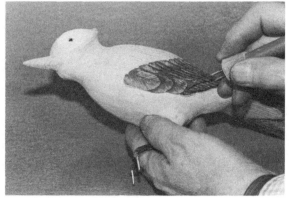

Figure 3-15c & d   Feather texturing with a burning pen.

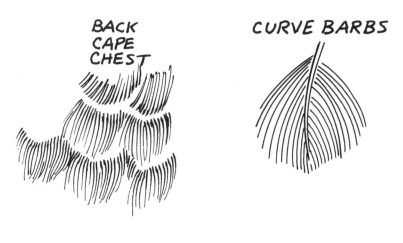

BACK
CAPE
CHEST

CURVE BARBS

SCAPULARS

VERMICULATION

BACK

Figure 3-15e   Feather textures.

Many carvers prefer to file down the tip of the pen so that it resembles more of a knife edge. Take care, though, if you clamp the pen in a vise to work on it; the heating element in many pens is enclosed in ceramic material, which is easily cracked. Don't put pressure on the point of your pen when burning—let the heat do the work. Make it a habit to wipe the burning edge often with a piece of coarse steel wool to keep it free from burned residue. A little practice will make you proficient in the use of this handy tool.

Carver's mark

Throughout history, when human beings created something in which they took pride, they placed their mark on it. It might be their initials, or perhaps a symbol that would set it aside as being their work. In the old West this took the form of the brand, which, applied to cattle, tools, and equipment, signified ownership. Industry, recognizing the value of instant recognition of quality products, was quick to adopt the idea in the form of trademarks. We are all familiar with the bell the telephone company uses, the many emblems the car manufacturers use, and the host of designs that readily identify the items we use in everyday life.

Why not work out a carver's mark to apply to your carvings? Your initials can be worked into a simple design that will be both distinctive and pleasing to the eye. A well-known sculptor, famous for his works in bronze depicting men and animals of the old West, uses a buffalo skull as his mark. Just as artists sign their paintings, it seems altogether fitting that woodcarvers should apply their mark to their work.

You can make a logotype of your initials simpy by bending a piece of stiff wire into the desired shape. By heating it with a propane torch or on the burner of your kitchen stove, your initials can be burned into the bottom of your carving. This branding iron can be inserted into a wooden handle, or it can be held with a pair of pliers to prevent burning your hand. Custom-made branding irons may be purchased for this same purpose.

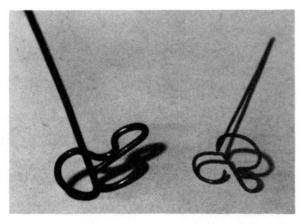

Figure 3-16a   Homemade branding iron.

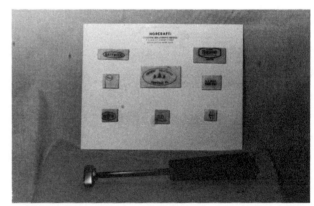

Figure 3-16b & c   Custom-made branding irons.

The greatest thing that can be said for power tools is that they are time-savers. If you find, like most of us, that you must acquire power tools slowly over a period of years due to the expense entailed, a good choice for a first power tool will be a band saw. Don't, however, consider one with less than a 12-inch throat.

A scroll saw will come in mighty handy if you get into finework. Good ones with a 15-inch throat are on the market and are not too expensive.

A flexible-shaft or motor grinder tool has many uses and can easily remove large quantities of wood in a short time.

Flexi-sanders with brush-backed abrasive strips will quickly smooth various shapes and can be used with an electric motor or chucked into a portable electric drill.

We cannot leave the subject of power tools without mentioning the extreme importance of safety measures. Don't work around power tools wearing a necktie or with loose shirt sleeves. Make it a practice to wear safety goggles when operating power grinders, saws, drills, or lathes. Sears has an excellent pair that are side ventilated and so designed that they can be worn over eyeglasses. Remember, a pair of safety goggles is a lot cheaper than a Seeing Eye dog!

Figure 3-17 "Spike" Boyd, master woodcarver, works with power hand tools and safety goggles.

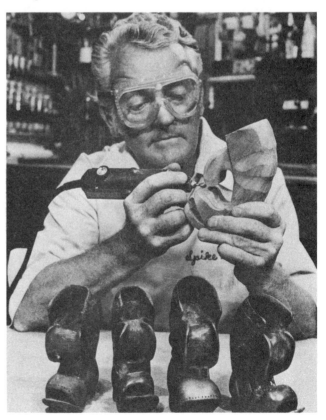

Another good practice is to wear a dust mask if doing band-sawing, power-sanding, or working with a hand grinder or flexible-shaft tool. If you find yourself getting tired, stop working and do something else for a while. Fatigue leads to carelessness and poor workmanship.

The workbench

The importance of a good sturdy workbench cannot be over-emphasized. It should be of solid construction and be well lighted. Fluorescent workshop fixtures that are chain-hung for adjustability are ideal. Make sure that electrical outlets are well situated in relation to the workbench, and mount your vise securely on the corner where your right hand will be when you face the workbench. Wall-mounted tool racks or a pegboard will be of great help in keeping your tools accessible. Also provide a kitchen or bar stool.

Plans for two convenient variations on the traditional workbench—a carving bench and a lap bench—follow.

Carving bench

This bench is designed to provide a convenient, comfortable work area for you to sit and do your carving in a limited space. The bench shown was designed by the author; however, many variations of the basic bench can be made to suit

Figure 3-18   Two examples of a carving bench.

your individual neeeds. Mr. Elmer Jumper, of the Pennsylvania Delaware Valley Woodcarvers, has designed a unique collapsible form of the bench, making it convenient to carry to and from shows and club meetings. One form even includes a removable vise to hold your carving.

Lap bench

In the event that you do not have space for a full shop or full-sized workbench, a very inexpensive and convenient lap bench can be constructed from the plans in Figure 3-19. This lap bench can make it possible for you to carve and enjoy the company of your family at the same time. With the flexibility of this bench, many operations can be accomplished, including the sawing out of basic blanks with the jigsaw accessory designed to use a hand coping saw. The bench is so designed that not only may you use it on your lap but it can also be used on a table by hooking the front edge over the table. A rubber backing protects the tabletop from damage.

Vise

A good vise is a lifetime investment, so purchase a sturdy one with at least a 6-inch jaw opening. Bolt it securely to the corner of your workbench; you will find it will come in handy for much use other than woodcarving. From scrap pegboard or hardboard cut 2 pieces to fit inside the jaws. This will enable your carving to be clamped securely without being marred.

Carver's screw

This carver's screw and others like it are available from good carving supply houses. One of the best on the market (shown in Fig. 3-20) is manufactured by Cliff Huston, of Philadelphia (see appendix). This convenient device is used to hold your carving in a rigid position, thus leaving both hands free to carve. Insert the point of the screw into the base of your carving block. Remove the wing nut and pass the other end through a hole in a board; then replace the wing nut and tighten it against the bottom of the board. Clamp the entire unit in your vise and start carving.

Figure 3-19   Carver's lap bench.
Designed by Elmer Jumper.

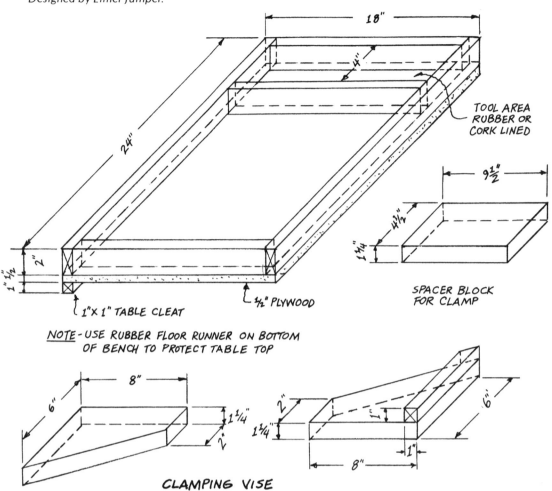

18"

4"

24"

TOOL AREA
RUBBER OR
CORK LINED

2"

1½"

1" X 1" TABLE CLEAT

½" PLYWOOD

9½"

4½"

1¾"

SPACER BLOCK
FOR CLAMP

<u>NOTE</u> - USE RUBBER FLOOR RUNNER ON BOTTOM
OF BENCH TO PROTECT TABLE TOP

8"

6"

1¼"

2"

2"

1¼"

1"

6"

1"

8"

CLAMPING VISE

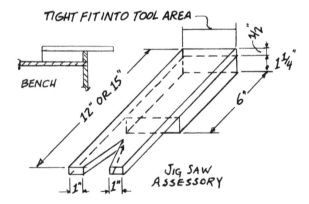

TIGHT FIT INTO TOOL AREA

½"

1¼"

12" OR 15"

6"

BENCH

1"   1"

JIG SAW
ASSESSORY

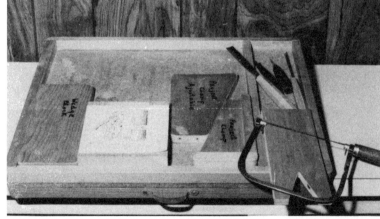

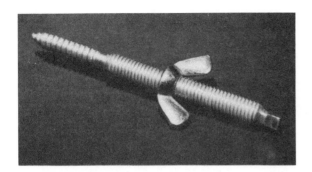

Figure 3-20   Carver's screw.

Carving fixture

In order to hold your carving in a convenient position, a simple fixture fashioned from scrap wood and a carver's screw or similar holding screw can be made (plans follow). By securely fastening the fixture in your bench vise and fastening the carving to the top plate with the screw, the carving can be rotated into a convenient carving position. Many variations of this device can be designed by you to suit your individual needs.

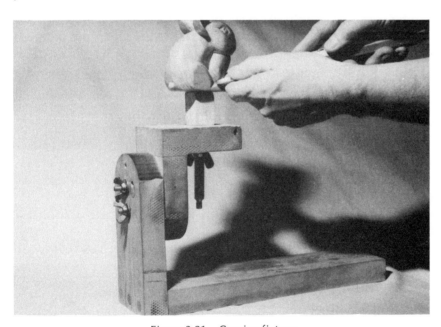

Figure 3-21   Carving fixture.

Holding stick

A holding stick, often called a third hand, will be worth its weight in gold. It is simple to make, and you will find it will come in handy for much use in both carving and painting your carvings. To make one for small carvings, cut a piece of

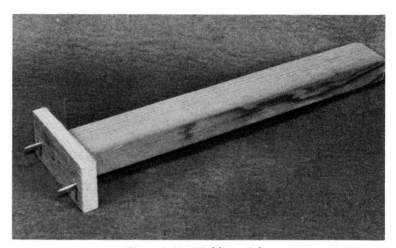

Figure 3-22   Holding stick.

scrap wood 16 inches long by 1½ inches wide by ¾-inch thick. To one end epoxy-glue a piece 2½ inches by 1¼ inches wide by ⅜-inch thick to form a *T*. A short distance from each end of the top of the T, drill holes to accommodate two ¾-inch roundheaded screws. These screws will be driven up through the bottom of the carving to hold it securely. The holding stick can be clamped in a vise at any angle and will hold your carving, enabling you to have both hands free to use rasps and carving tools. Large holding sticks can be made to these proportions to handle larger carvings.

4

Aids and accessories

In addition to the tools, there are a great many aids that can be of tremendous help in carving. We'll review a few of them in the hope that they will further you on your path to becoming a better woodcarver. Some of these aids can be purchased, others can be simply made from scrap and material from your workshop.

From time to time you will see a particular object that you would like to reproduce in a woodcarving. In order to determine the specific dimensions and transfer them to a pattern, several devices can easily be made from scrap wood or can be purchased commercially.

Transferring measurements from a model to a pattern

Proportional dividers

While standard dividers are designed to transfer an equal measurement from a fixed object or plan, proportional dividers are designed to translate a measurement into an enlargement or reduction of the original size. Thus, when the proportional divider is preset at a given percentage, all measurements will automatically be reduced or enlarged by moving the pivot point up or down. If an enlargement is needed, a reading is taken with the smaller end; if a reduction is needed, a reading is taken with the larger end. The home-

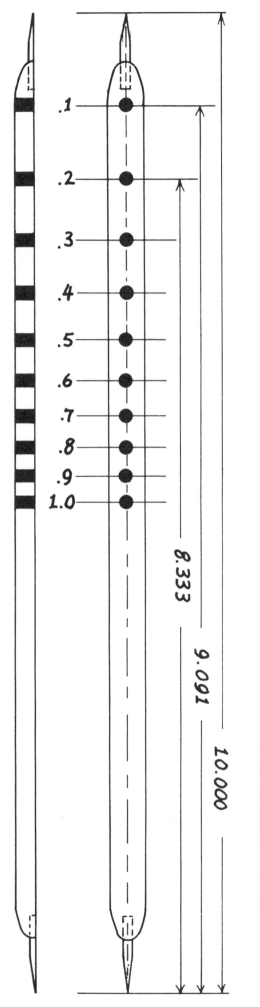

.1

.2

.3

.4

.5

.6

.7

.8

.9

1.0

8.333

9.091

10.000

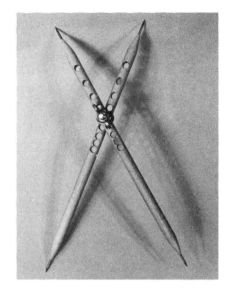

Figure 4-1   Proportion dividers.

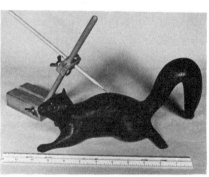

Figure 4-2   Proportion scale.

Figure 4-3   Thickness calipers.

Figure 4-4   The vertical gauge.

made pair of dividers shown in Figure 4-1a were made from thin, hard wood sticks from the plans shown in Figure 4-1b. A common finishing nail was used to form the points. Although not mathematically correct, they will produce a very satisfactory translation of a plan to a rough percentage of that desired. A simple bolt and wing nut were used as the pivot and tightening device.

Proportion scale

This carving aid will translate your measurements into a reduced or enlarged size and can be obtained from a good drafting supply store. By rotating the scale and aligning the measurement from the original object with the desired finished size, a percentage of the reduction or enlargement can be determined. By leaving the scale at this set position, each new measurement from your original object can easily be converted to the finished size.

Once each of the individual readings from the original object have been determined and then transferred to a sheet of paper, a reasonable reproduction can be drawn by filling in the lines between the points.

Thickness calipers

With this simple pair of calipers, the thickness of a given point on an object can be measured and the reading transferred to the finished object or plan. The caliper is constructed by cutting two equal-size arcs from thin plywood and fastening them together with a standard bolt and wing nut for tightening purposes.

Vertical gauge

To determine a given point on an object in its relation to the horizontal plane, this adjustable gauge can be placed at a given point on the object and a measurement taken in relation to the flat surface on which the object is standing. The gauge is constructed from scrap wood and standard dowels using bolts and wing nuts as tightening devices. By taking numerous readings from the original model and transferring them to a plan, a satisfactory reproduction can be made.

Total-length gauge

The total length of certain odd-shaped objects cannot be accurately measured with an ordinary tape measure, but by simply placing the vertical posts of this special tool at the extreme ends of the object, a true reading can be attained. The

Figure 4-5   Total-length gauge

gauge shown in Figure 4-5 is very simply constructed as the vertical gauge is, from standard dowel rods glued to two pieces of scrap lumber that serve as bases to hold the rods upright.

Reference materials

You will also want to have ready access to reference materials—books or charts that show birds and animals in full color and various poses, a reference file of pictures from publications, and a source where you can obtain or observe mounted models of stuffed specimens.

The reference file

Every carver should have a reference file; we call it the carver's friend. If you don't have one, this would be a good time to start. The first reference file was contained in an old wooden ginger ale case. Eventually it grew larger and graduated to a two-drawer filing cabinet. As a starter, obtain an old corrugated liquor carton from your friendly spirits store—it's just the right size. Covered with printed adhesive-backed paper of a wood-grain pattern, it will do very well.

Get yourself a pack of 11¾-by 9½-inch tabbed manila folders, and, with a marking pen, label the tabs with the various subjects you are interested in carving. They might be labeled as follows: Songbirds, Waterfowl, Birds of Prey, Game Birds, Horses, Dogs, Animals, Fish, Figures, Toys, Ships, Flowers, Designs, Alphabet Initials, Carbon Paper, Tracing Paper, and so on.

Magazines such as *National Wildlife, Field and Stream, National Geographic,* and so on will soon provide a wealth of pictures for clipping. Ask your friends to pass on their old magazines to you. Many times such periodicals can be picked up at a flea market or secondhand bookshop at small cost. Our file is not too old, yet it can furnish a dozen or so pictures of any bird or subject we wish to carve. They are especially helpful when a question of a pose arises. And, of course, being able to refer to color pictures when it comes to painting your carvings is invaluable.

On pages 40 and 41 is a list of reference materials available from the Pennsylvania Game Commission. Send your request to: Pennsylvania Game Commission, P.O. Box 1567, Harrisburg, Pennsylvania 17120.

Bird charts

Bird carvers will be glad to know that many states furnish charts of songbirds, waterfowl, and animals native to their state in full color at nominal cost (figures 4-6a–c). The U.S. Government also has publications of this sort available. Your local library can furnish many excellent reference books for your use.

PENNSYLVANIA GAME COMMISSION
BIRD AND MAMMAL CHARTS
By Nationally Known Wildlife Artist NED SMITH

SET NO. 1 (20" x 30")— $4 delivered
Winter Birds, Marsh and Water Birds, Waterfowl, Birds of Prey
SET NO. 2 (20" x 30")— $4 delivered
Mammals of Farm and Woodlot, Mammals of the Mountains, Birds of the Forest, Birds of Field and Garden
SET NO. 3 (11" x 14")— $4 delivered
All eight charts listed in Set No. 1 and Set No. 2
(Individual charts not sold in either size)
Make check or money order payable to
PENNSYLVANIA GAME COMMISSION
P. O. Box 1567, Harrisburg, Pa. 17120

Figure 4-6 Bird and mammal charts available through the Pennsylvania Game Commission.

39

BIRD AND MAMMAL CHARTS
  Size 20" × 30"
    Set #1 (4 charts)
    Set #2 (4 charts)
  Size 11" × 14"
    Set #3 (the 8 charts contained in sets #1 and #2)

SYMBOLS CHART (Shows State Animal, Bird, Tree, and Flower)

GAME NEWS COVER PRINTS (Consists of 4 11" × 14" colored prints: Doves, Buck and Doe, Woodcock, and Woodchuck)

BOOKS
  White-Tailed Deer (out of print)
  Mammals of Pennsylvania
  Pennsylvania Birdlife
  Ducks at a Distance

You can also order the following free literature from the Pennsylvania Game Commission:

American Woodcock in Pennsylvania

Beaver in Pennsylvania

Bronze Beauty of the Big Woods (Turkey)

Cottontail Rabbit

Duck Identification Chart

Keystone Bruin (Bear)

Meet the Squirrel Family

Opossum, a Look at the

Oriental Bombshell (Pheasant)

Pennyslvania Woodchuck

Ruffed Grouse

25 Well-known Pennsylvania Birds

25 Well-known Pennsylvania Mammals

Vanishing Spitfire (Wildcat)

Whistlin' Robert (Bobwhite Quail)

White-tailed Deer in Pennsylvania

Wildlife Notes (24 Pamplets) on:

Beaver	Cottontail Rabbit
Bobcat	Crows and Ravens
Bobwhite	Doves
Canada Goose	Foxes (red & gray)

Herron	Ruffed Grouse
Minks & Muskrats	Squirrels
Otter	Striped Skunk
Owls	Varying Hare
Porcupine	Wild Turkey
Raccoons	Woodchuck
Raptors	Woodpecker
Ring-necked Pheasants	Woodcock

Try it—you will find it well worth the effort!

Mounted models

We have found that no matter how accomplished the artist or photographer, two-dimensional representations can't compare with mounted subjects as far as body configuration and colors are concerned. Fortunately many museums will loan carvers and artists a mounted bird or animal for a small donation. Rod and gun clubs may also be willing to loan you mounted specimens once you have made known the fact that you are a woodcarver.

Aids to organize and care for tools, work area, and materials

Since most carvers have a very limited space in which to work, it is important to be well organized. We strongly advise that you plan the storage of your materials, the set-up of your work area, and a method of caring for your tools carefully so that you don't wind up being inundated, your equipment strewn about the bench. The following suggestions should aid you in overcoming this problem and increase your working pleasure.

A carrying case for small tools

To keep your small tools in order when transporting them to carving shows and meetings, a tool case will prove very convenient. An old attaché case can be converted into a handy carrying case by devising tool holders and a tray for knives and small items. Thin wooden dividers can be fashioned into a tray from slats of old Venetian blinds or from thin plywood to separate the tools. It goes without saying that all edged tools should have blade guards. In order to restrict the move-

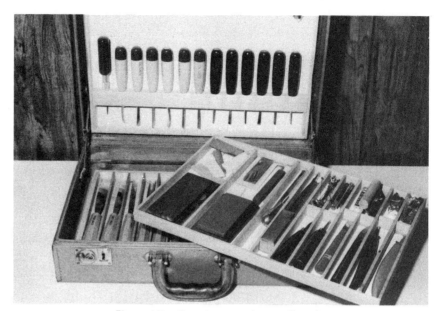

Figure 4-7   Carrying case for small tools.

ment of tools, a thin sheet of foam plastic should be placed between each level of the case.

Lazy Susan tool rack

This rotary tool rack offers four surfaces on which tools can be placed so that they'll be at your fingertips and readily accessible (Figure 4-8a). By making interchangeable boards, a large variety of tools can be positioned. For easy reading of patterns or reference books, one surface can be set aside to hold the drawing or book at eye level (Figure 4-8b). Your own variation of the unit can be made to suit your needs. A suitable cabinet base can also be constructed to provide you with additional drawer space for tools and supplies. Casters may be applied to the bottom for mobility.

Figure 4-8   Lazy Susan tool racks.

Figure 4-9   Wood storage rack.

Wood storage racks and bins

Storage racks and bins will be necessary for you will soon find that you have become addicted to wood hoarding (see Figure 4-9). Several cartons can be kept in your workshop to hold smaller pieces. Build racks along one of the interior walls of your garage to store various size lengths of the larger pieces. Green wood that is being cured is better stored in an unheated garage than in a heated cellar. Keep separate bins or cartons for driftwood bases, gnarled branches and roots for bird mounts, and shorter odds and ends.

Filler material

Epoxy putty

Epoxy putty has a great many uses, especially for bird carvers. It makes an excellent filler where the head joins the body on waterfowl, where outspread wings join the body, and where legs join the body. After it has been applied dip your fingertip in water and blend the putty into each piece being bonded. When painted, the joint will be invisible and the desired realistic appearance will be attained. Bear in mind, however, that epoxy putty will crumble if you attempt to texture it with a burning pen. Any texturing should be done with a sharp instrument while the putty is still wet. A cellulose filler material can be used in place of epoxy putty; this material is not water soluble but can be smoothed with a few drops of lacquer thinner. The cellulose filler can be textured with the burning pen as long as the pen is limited to a low setting.

5
Helpful hints

We'd like to round out this general discussion of how to get started in woodcarving by giving you a number of helpful hints that we have acquired during our carving years. If you are going into competition at carving shows, and you will as your skills improve, keep in mind that the way you present your finished carving will greatly affect your chances of winning that coveted ribbon. A bird or wildlife carving set in a natural mounting will attract the eye of the judges more than a carving mounted on a plain wooden base every time. Make use of gnarled roots and driftwood. Acorns are easily carved from wood, and fall leaves can be cut from grocery bag paper and carefully painted. Papier-mâché materials from a hobby shop can easily be molded into an interesting contour on your base. Keep away from plastic flowers and vinyl leaves. They do not add to your stature as a woodcarver.

Many helpful tips can be garnered by visiting woodcarving shows. Engage the exhibitors in conversation. Once they learn that you, too, are a woodcarver, they will be glad to share their knowledge with you.

Ever break a carving transporting it to a show-and-tell session at your club meeting or to a woodcarving show° Try wrapping your carved figures in tissue paper and inserting them into the individual cubbyholes of those cartons from the liquor store that have corrugated partition inserts.

Always make blade guards for your edged carving tools, both as a safety precaution and to keep those edges razor-sharp. A simple shield can be made from a piece of cardboard folded around the blade, then wrapped with several thicknesses of glass filament or plastic tape. These are easy to replace if lost, and they will do the job.

Several nail sets in various sizes will prove very handy in making eyes for your carvings. A word of caution, however: Don't tap them with a hammer or you will recess them too deeply. Instead, position the point of the nail set and, holding it in your hand, apply pressure as you twist it.

For getting into tight spots, common emery boards will fill the bill. They have a medium and a fine side and can be cut into odd shapes with a pair of scissors.

How to lay out a perfect oval

An oval base if often necessary to display your carving to its best advantage. Follow these simple instructions for a perfect oval base. Try it . . . it works every time!

Step 1: Draw cross lines to the center of the oval (Figure 5-1a).

Step 2: Fasten a string to two small brads or tacks equal to the largest diameter of the oval (Figure 5-1b). This determines the length of the string.

Step 3: Determine the tack locations by swinging half the string length from the smallest diameter of the oval (Figure 5-1c).

Step 4: Fix the end tacks in their location. With a pencil inside the string, draw your perfect oval (Figure 5-1d).

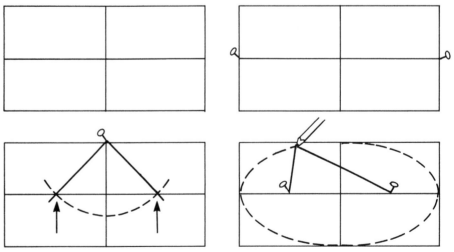

Figure 5-1 a-d   How to lay out a perfect oval.

How to glue up wood

Many carving projects, such as a sperm whale or life-sized ducks and geese, will call for such thickness in wood that several pieces must be glued together. If the subject is to be painted, a good glued joint will be impossible to detect. Position the pieces of wood so that the grain runs in the same direction, making sure that the surfaces to be glued are perfectly flat. Use a good grade of glue, such as Franklin's Titebond or Elmer's Carpenters Glue. Clamp up tightly with as many clamps as you can use. Wipe away any oozed-out glue with a damp rag, and let set in a warm, dry place overnight.

Try to remind yourself to make frequent use of a shop vacuum. Your family may love you dearly, but a trail of chips and sawdust across the living room rug will not exactly endear you or your hobby to their hearts!

6
Making patterns

Unless you are an accomplished artist, which most of us are not, before you begin to carve you will need a pattern, that is, a side view and a top view of the same dimensions in order to outline your carving subject on your block of wood.

You can make your own patterns based on pictures of your chosen subject from your reference file. They can be made on tracing paper and transfered to the wood with carbon paper; however, since you will probably use them many times, it will be best if you trace them onto heavy cardboard first, then cut them out carefully. For example, you can make a decoy pattern with a basic body and several different positions of the head and neck. This will enable you to carve a duck with its head at the alert position, tilted up with bill open, head stretched out as in feeding, or head tucked in with the bill touching the breast. If you are carving a pair of ducks, it will be desirable to have the heads in different positions.

Often it will be necessary to make your carving larger or smaller than your original pattern. This can be accomplished by using one of the following: a grid sheet, a pantograph, a rubber-band enlarger, or a projector.

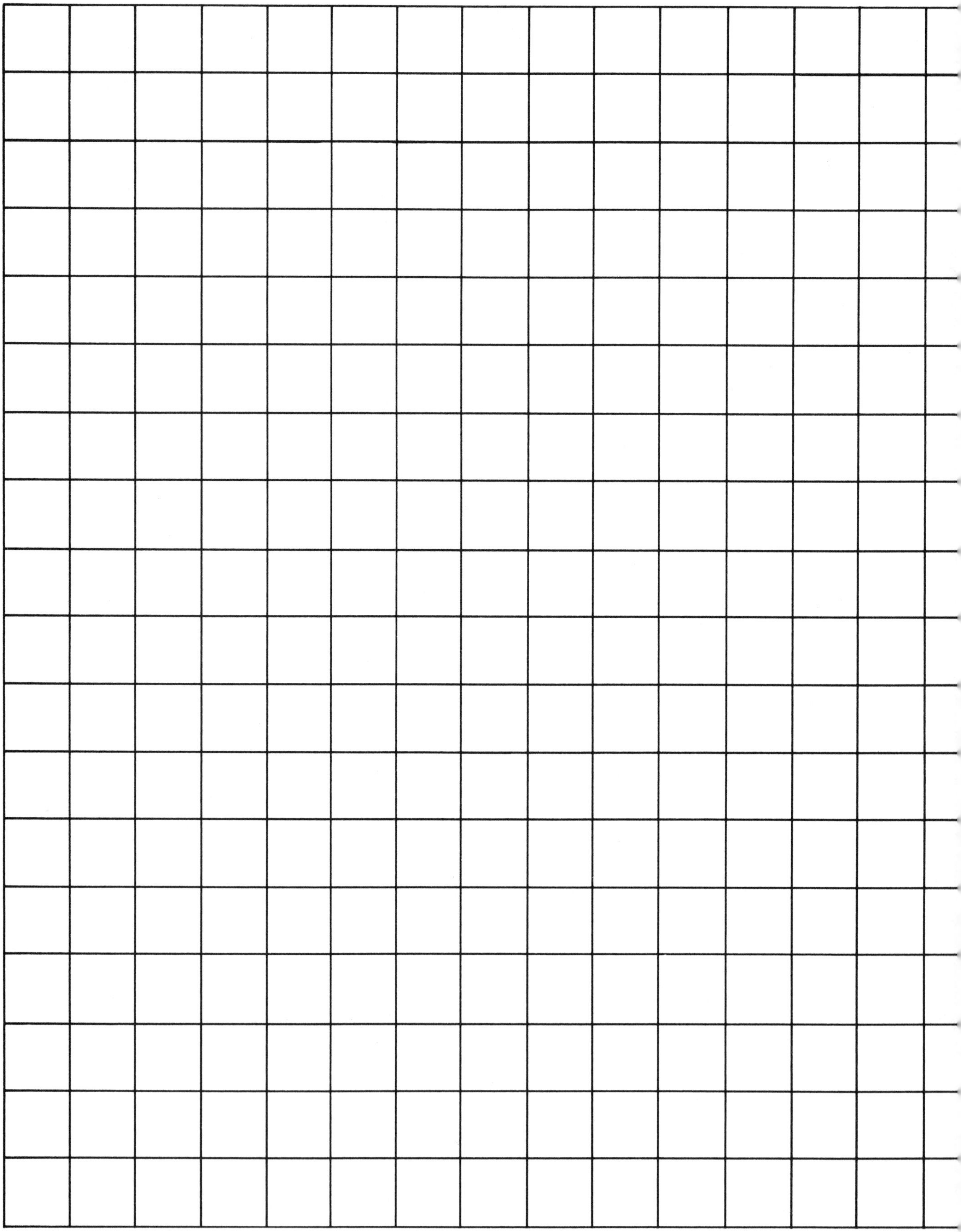

Figure 6-1   Sample grid.

How to use a grid sheet

If you wish to enlarge or reduce the size of a plan, simply transfer the grid sheet to tracing paper and place it over the drawing. Then rule a separate sheet of paper with either larger or smaller squares. Very carefully transfer each line of the drawing that appears in a particular square to your new grid sheet (Figure 6-2). This will give you a very satisfactory reproduction of the original.

How to use a pantograph

The pantograph is a very useful instrument and can be acquired inexpensively from any good art store. With it pictures or patterns can either be reproduced the same size, reduced, or enlarged. When you have determined how many times you want to reduce or enlarge the original, set the adjusting knobs, clamp the one end of the instrument securely to your drawing surface, and with masking tape, fasten down both the original pattern and the paper on which your reproduction is to be reproduced. Then simply trace the original pattern with the stylus.

Rubber band enlarger

A very simple device, designed by a carver unknown to us, is shown in Figures 6-4a and b. It will enlarge an original drawing to exactly twice its size. Unfortunately, this device is limited in its use and cannot be used to obtain other-size enlargements, as can other tools designed for this purpose. It is composed of two equal-sized rubber bands and a small square of clear sheet plastic. A small cross line is inscribed in the center of the plastic sheet and a darkening agent rubbed into the lines to intensify them. A 3/16″ hole is then drilled in each end. A rubber band is passed through each hole and looped back on itself, pulled tight to hold it firmly in place. The enlarger is then operated by fastening one loop of one rubber band to a board with a thumb tack, then drawing a diagonal line out from the point of the tack. Place the original drawing on the diagonal line just about at a point where a bit of tension on both rubber bands causes the crossed lines to fall on the diagonal line. Fasten the original in place at this point with tape. Place the point of your pencil in the loop of the loose rubber band and increase tension until the cross lines are aligned with the original image. By using the pull on the rubber band as a force, move the cross

Figure 6-2　How to use a grid sheet.

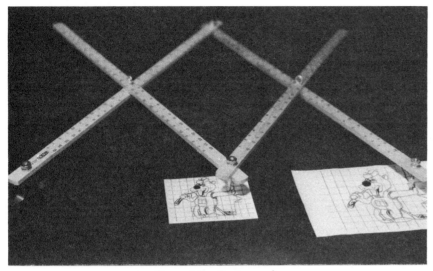

Figure 6.3   Pantograph.

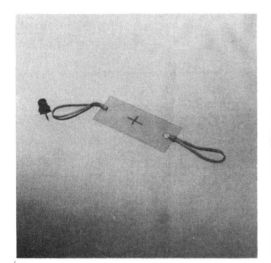

Figure 6-4 a & b   Rubber band enlarger.

line over the original very carefully and your pencil will do the rest. The result will be admittedly a very crude reproduction, but with care the lines can be redrawn to give you a satisfactory pattern.

How to use a projector

If you possess a 35mm camera and a projector, you have the means of enlarging or reducing patterns very simply. Take photos of the side and top views of your subject and have them made up into slides. Tape a piece of paper onto a vertical surface and project the slides onto it. Adjust the projected picture to the desired size and draw the outline

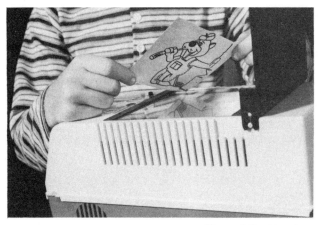

Figure 6-5   How to use an opaque projector.

you see on your paper screen with a pencil. An opaque projecter can be used in much the same way (see Figure 6-5).

Making patterns from an existing object

At times you will come across a special item that you would like to reproduce in wood, such as a fine ceramic animal or some similar item. A very satisfactory reproduction can be made by making a vertical reproduction gauge. First fasten a sheet of stiff cardboard in a slot cut into a block of wood. The front and bottom are to be at a perfect 90 degree angle to each other. On the side of the cardboard, devise a holding clamp that will hold a pencil at about a 45 degree angle to the bottom corner of the cardboard. The holding device shown in the illustration is just a grooved block of wood held tightly to the card with a bolt and wing nut. Move the pencil down until the point extends just to the tip of the bottom corner so that if moved across a sheet of paper it will make a mark. Place the item to be copied in position on your paper. Now very carefully move the device around the object to be copied, being very careful not to allow the object to move at any time. If done correctly you should have a very satisfactory top view of the item.

To create a side view of the object it is necessary that the object be positioned with its base at a 90 degree angle to the paper. To accomplish this, another simple device must be fashioned from scrap wood. Some form of clamping device must also be made to hold it in this position. By fastening two flat boards together at 90 degrees and attaching a clamping

(a)

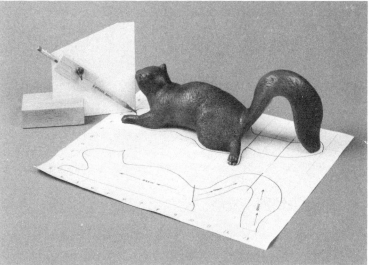

(b)

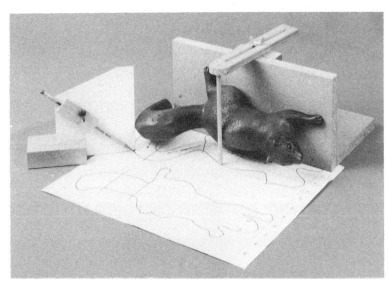

(c)

device, a very satisfactory base can be made that will hold the object. If you take your vertical gauge as before and move it around the contour of the object, you'll have a splendid set of two view plans from which to cut out your blank for carving. To further improve the plan, should you wish to reduce or enlarge it, refer to the grid method discussed earlier in this chapter. Simply draw the rulings on your plan with an equal-size grid and proceed as indicated.

Making patterns of the human figure

When you want to make patterns of the human figure, a set of movable-joint manikins will prove most helpful in visualizing a pose. From the front and side patterns illustrated in Figure 6-6b, simply trace the various body components—head, torso, upper arm, lower arm, and so on—onto a piece of firm fiberboard. Cut out and fasten the parts together with roundheaded brass paper fasteners, and you will have a little man that you can position in any possible manner. The manikins are particularly helpful in making a pattern of a figure in action—a person running, chopping wood, and so forth.

A more sophisticated wooden manikin, which can be purchased from a good art supply store, will give you a better three-dimensional perspective of the human figure should you care to make a more expensive investment.

Once you have your patterns, it's a good idea to file them in the correct folder of your reference file, which will enable you to have your patterns, poses, and data about coloring at your fingertips.

Now that you have your pattern, you can proceed with your carving using one of the carving techniques described in the next chapter.

Figure 6-7a   Set of movable-joint manikins.

Figure 6-7b   Wooden manikin.
Photo courtesy Kromschnabel Studios.

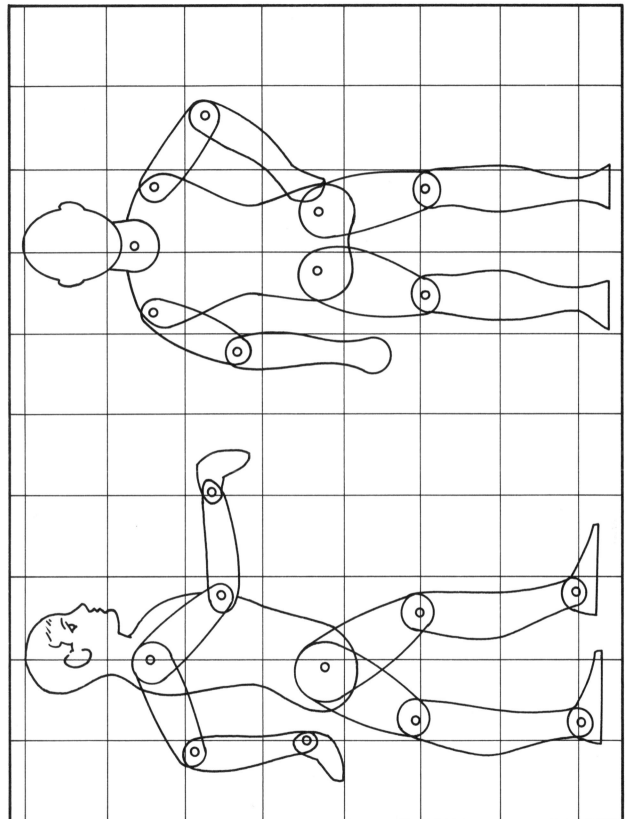

Figure 6-7c   Patterns for making manikins.

Techniques of woodcarving

Line carving

Often called the simplest form of carving, line carving is an ideal project for the beginner. In line carving the outlined subject and the background remain at the original surface level of the panel being carved. By making practice cuts on a piece of scrap of the same wood being carved, you will get the feel of working with chisels and gouges and will experience what can be accomplished working both with and across the grain with sharp tools. By making a series of short cuts with your tool, better control will be maintained. Select a pattern that appeals to you from the following pages and go to it.

The ten steps of line carving are as follows:

1. Cut a panel to the desired finished size.

2. Sand the face and edges smooth.

3. Draw border lines that will frame the completed carving.

4. Transfer the image to be carved to your prepared panel using carbon paper, making sure that the image fits within the predetermined border limits.

5. With a V- or U-shaped gouge, cut a shallow groove in each of the lines of the pattern. Care should be taken to control the gouge from slipping too fast foward. This can be done by holding the gouge with the left hand just above the cutting edge and exerting a reverse pressure to control its forward motion.

6. When the carving has been compelted, lightly sand the surface of the panel to remove any splinters or fuzz. With a soft brush remove all of the sanding dust from all of the depressions.

7. Apply a coat of good wood sealer to the panel. We prefer a product called Sanding Sealer. The sealer will prevent any color material you may want to use to highlight the image from bleeding into the surrounding areas. Be sure to work the sealer down into the depressions to prevent any undercut bleeding. Be certain, however, to brush any excess from the grooves with a dry brush in order to keep from filling in the image and keep your color material from getting into the background area.

8. When the sealer has dried completely, work the color of your choice into the depressions.

9. When the color has dried completely, sand the face of the panel until all excess color has been removed. Once more dust out all excess sanding dust from the depressions.

10. Now finish the entire panel with a varnish of your choice or apply a good paste wax and buff to a good finish.

Figure 7-1a   Line carving of American elk.

Figure 7-2a   Line carving of mallard.

Figure 7-1b   Pattern for American elk.
Reprinted with permission of National Wildlife Federation.

Figure 7-2b   Pattern for mallard.
Reprinted with permission of National Wildlife Federation.

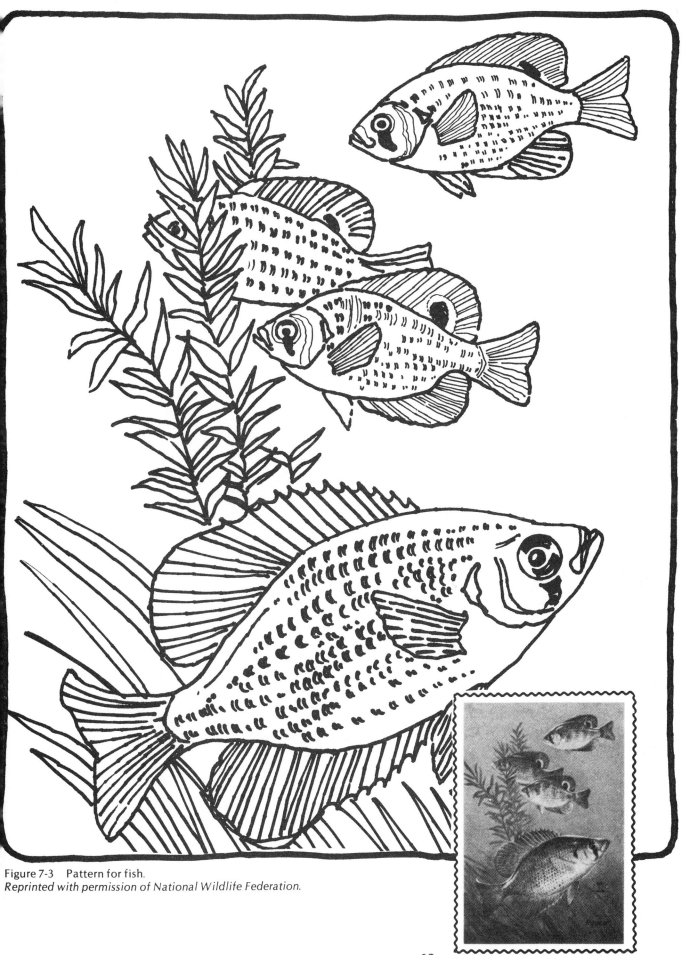

Figure 7-3   Pattern for fish.
Reprinted with permission of National Wildlife Federation.

Figure 7-4   Pattern for black-footed ferret.
Reprinted with permission of National Wildlife Federation.

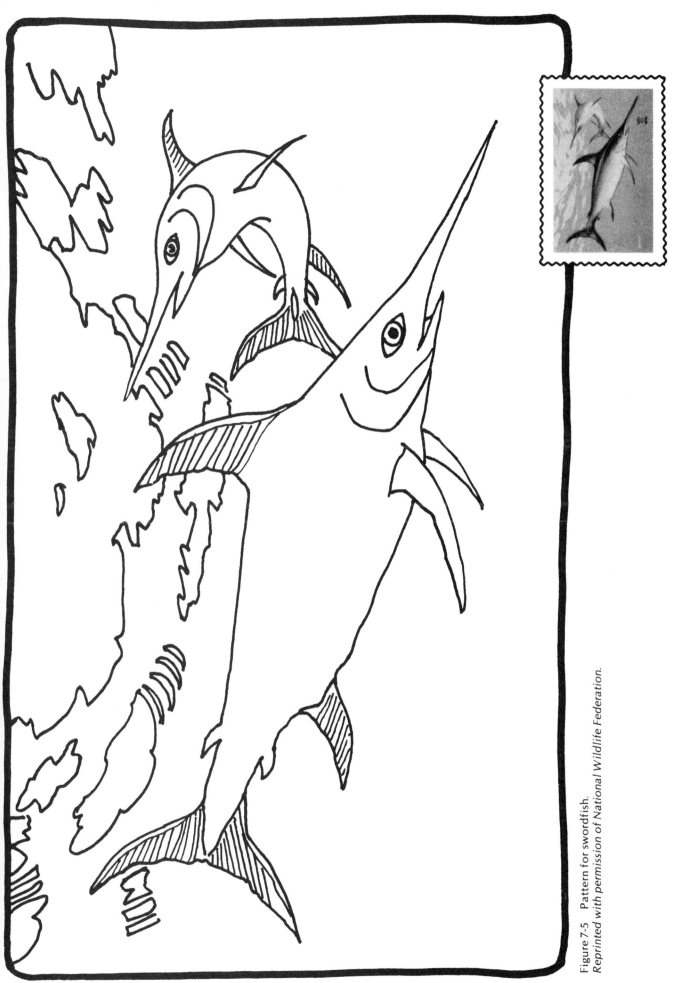

Figure 7-5   Pattern for swordfish.
Reprinted with permission of National Wildlife Federation.

Figure 7-6   Pattern for green heron.
Reprinted with permission of National Wildlife Federation.

Figure 7-7 Pattern for eastern chipmunk.
Reprinted with permission of National Wildlife Federation.

Figure 7-8   Pattern for turtle cartoon.

Figure 7-9   Pattern for snake cartoon.

Relief carving

A relief carving results in a pictorial representation of an object, a scene, or a portrait. This is achieved by making indentations in the wood in a three-dimensional manner, using chisels of varying shapes and sizes. However, much of the work can be accomplished with the use of a knife and basic carving tools. Before starting to carve, it is advisable to take your knife or chisel and cut vertical cuts on the pattern lines. These cuts are referred to as stop cuts (see Chapter 3). This prevents splitting and keeps the pattern vertical until that area is completed. There are really no specific steps to follow in this form of carving, as the carver does not work in or complete a specific area. Your first and foremost consideration should be to complete the highest point on the carving, such as a nose or forehead. Generally speaking, the carving must be viewed as a whole and the carver begins to get the feel of the need to remove a bit of wood here and a little there. Each area is cut as it relates to its adjacent area, progressing downward to the deepest sections of the picture. It is good practice to rough out the general picture and then go back and complete the details. This allows for adjustment and correction.

Figure 7-10a   Unfinished relief carving of Abraham Lincoln.

Figure 7-10b   Completed relief carving of Abraham Lincoln.

Figure 7-10c   Pattern for relief carving of Abraham Lincoln.

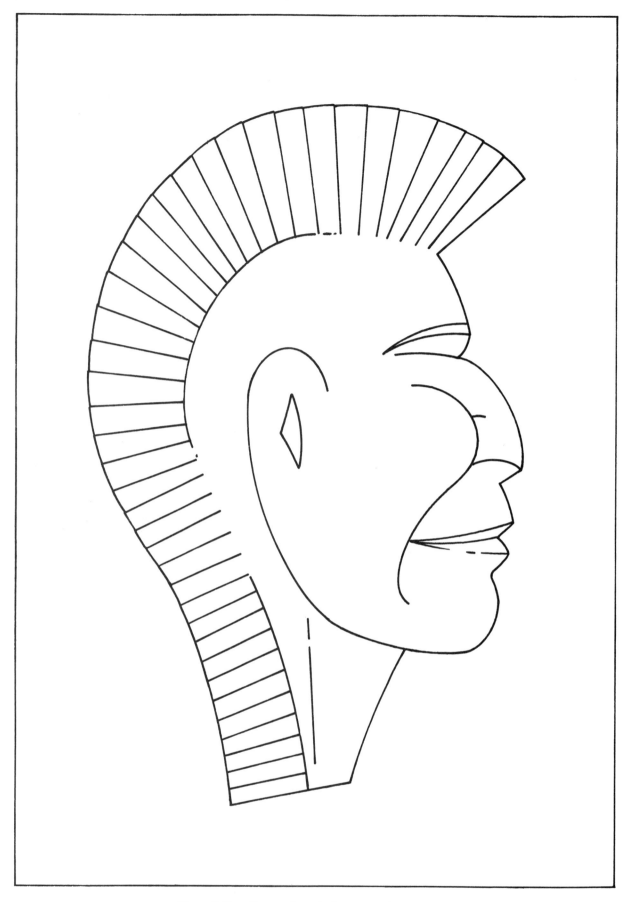

Figure 7-11a   Pattern for relief carving of Indian head.

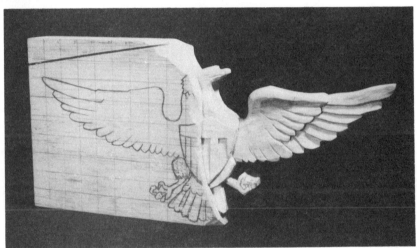

Figure 7-11b   Relief carving of Indian head.

Figure 7-12   Unfinished relief carving of eagle emblem.

Figure 7-13   Relief carving of trout.

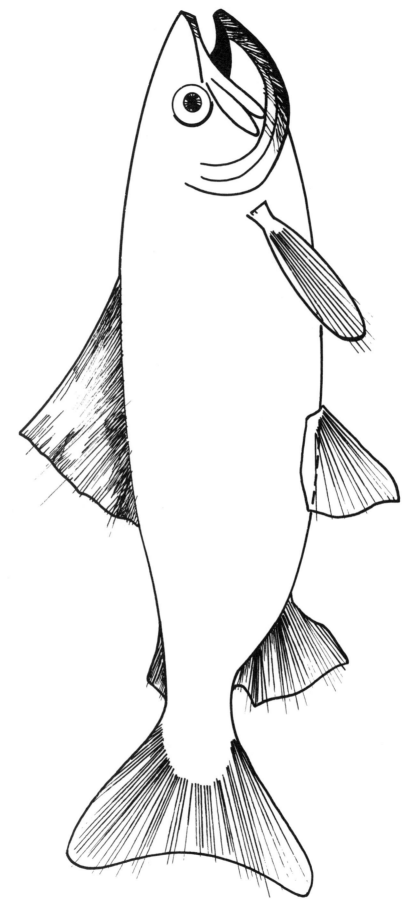

Figure 7-13b   Pattern for relief carving of trout.

Figure 7-14a   Unfinished relief carving of bear.

Figure 7-14b   Completed relief carving of bear.

Figure 7-14c   Pattern for relief carving of bear.

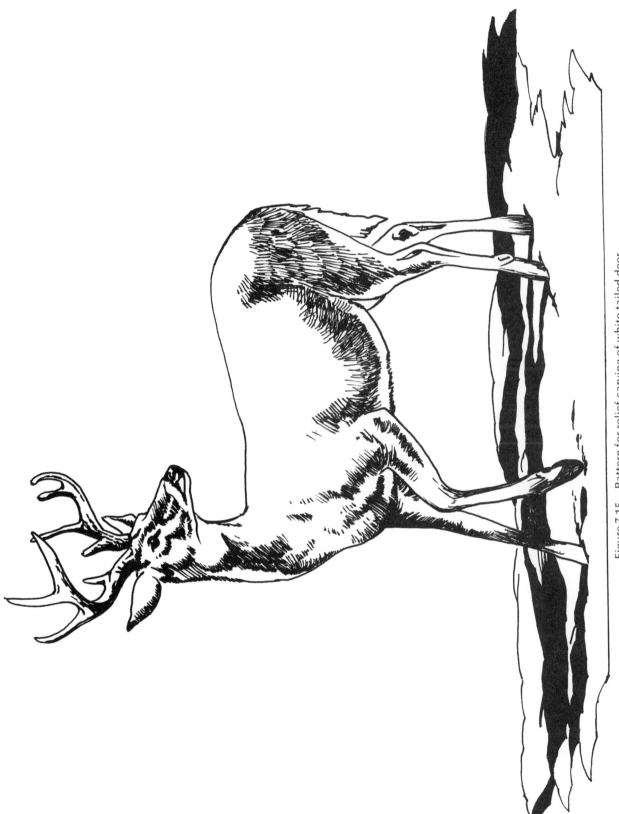

Figure 7-15 Pattern for relief carving of white-tailed deer.

Figure 7-16 Pattern for relief carving of covered bridge.

Figure 7-17   Pattern for relief carving of floral design.
Courtesy of Le Trimble.

Figure 7-18a   *Pattern for relief carving of Indian brave.*
Contributed by Elfred Atkinson.

Figure 7-18b   Pattern for relief carving of Indian maiden.
Contributed by Elfred Atkinson.

Carving in the round

Carving in the round is a designation given a subject that is carved on all sides, as opposed to the flat carving in line and relief carving where just the surface is carved. Patterns for in-the-round carving should include at least a side and front view. Depending upon the subject, an additional rear and top view are helpful in determining the details in these areas. This is especially true in carving animals and the human figure.

The following are the basic steps to be observed:—

1. Select a straight-grained block of wood that has been squared off with 90 degree angles. The block should be at least ½" longer than the finished carving.

2. Carefully transfer the side view of the pattern to the block with carbon paper or a cardboard cut-out of the pattern.

3. Placing a carpenter's try square along the edge of the block, scribe a pencil line across the short edge of the side view, crossing the last point of the pattern. Again, using the try square, continue this line across the other surface of the block. Place the front view of the pattern on this line. You will now have both the side and front views properly positioned on the block. It is advisable to draw a center line in pencil of the front view from top to bottom. With a band saw or a hand coping saw, carefully cut out the side profile in two pieces. For example, in the carving of Scotty, start sawing at the crown of the head, continue down the back of the head, the back, the back of the legs to the heel of the shoes keeping this sawed portion in one piece.

   Similarly, saw down the front of the figure, again keeping the sawed portion in one piece.

4. Reassemble all the cut off pieces back into a block form. With masking tape, tape them together, taking care that all points are lined up.

5. Now saw the front pattern. When sawing, always saw ⅟₃₂ nd" on the outside of the scribed pattern to allow for a little extra carving wood.

6. You will now have a squared-off blank of your subject. With a surform file or rasp, round off the squared corners.

7. With sharp tools, begin to carve in the details. Do not work in just one area of the carving but rather move about, doing some work on the head, body, and feet in order to get a better idea of proportion as they relate to each other.

8. Your finished carving may now be painted or stained, or a simple wax finish may be applied.

Painting Instructions for "Scotty" . . . . . Hat—Navy blue with red tourrie; clan badge, silver. Face, knees, hands, ruddy; hair, moustache, white. Jacket, stockings—gray. Over-the-shoulder plaid, tie, and kilt—Black Watch or any desirable tartan (shown in photo, Clan Johnston tartan). Sporran—black silver-mounted top, white horsehair, black hair tassels. Garter flashes—red.

Shoes—black with silver buckles.
Glue crooked walking stick to right hand.
Note: Front of kilt is unpleated where it overlaps.

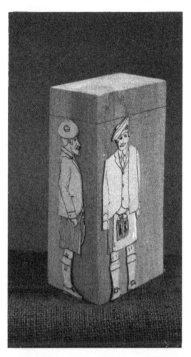

Figure 7-19a   Initial stage of carving-in-the-round of "Scotty"

Figure 7-19b   Four stages of carving-in-the-round of "Scotty"

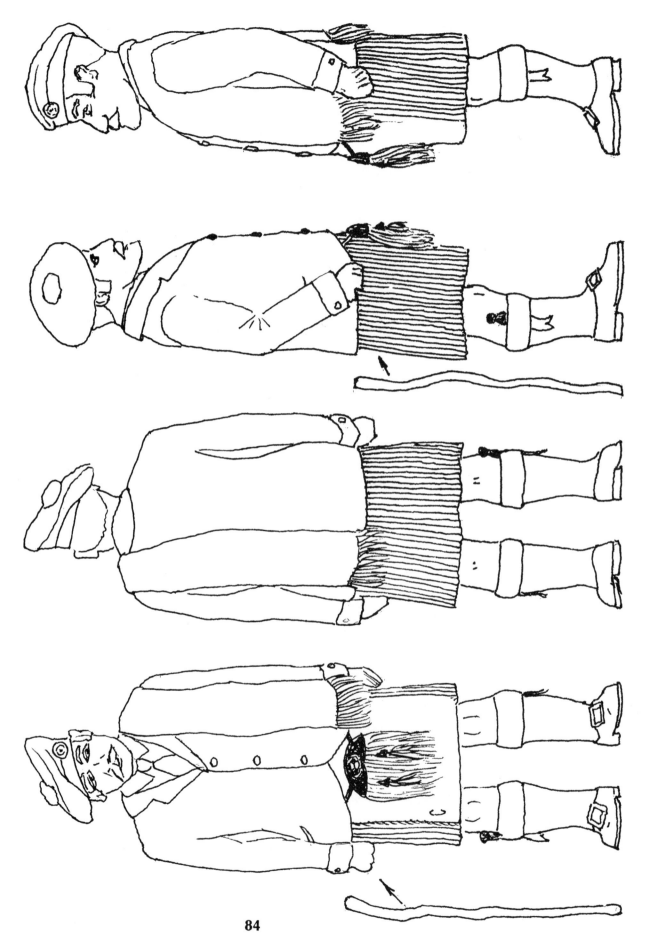

Figure 7–19C   Front, back, and side view pattern for carving-in-the-round of "Scotty"

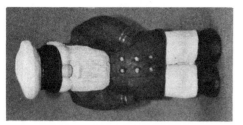

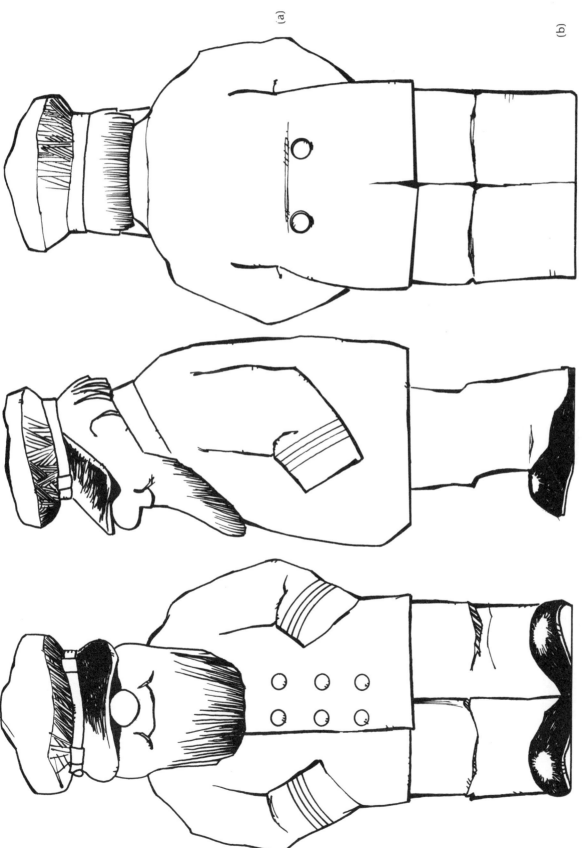

Figure 7-20   (a) Carving-in-the-round of the Cap'n, and (b) front-, side-, and back-view carving patterns. *Courtesy of Tom Koons.*

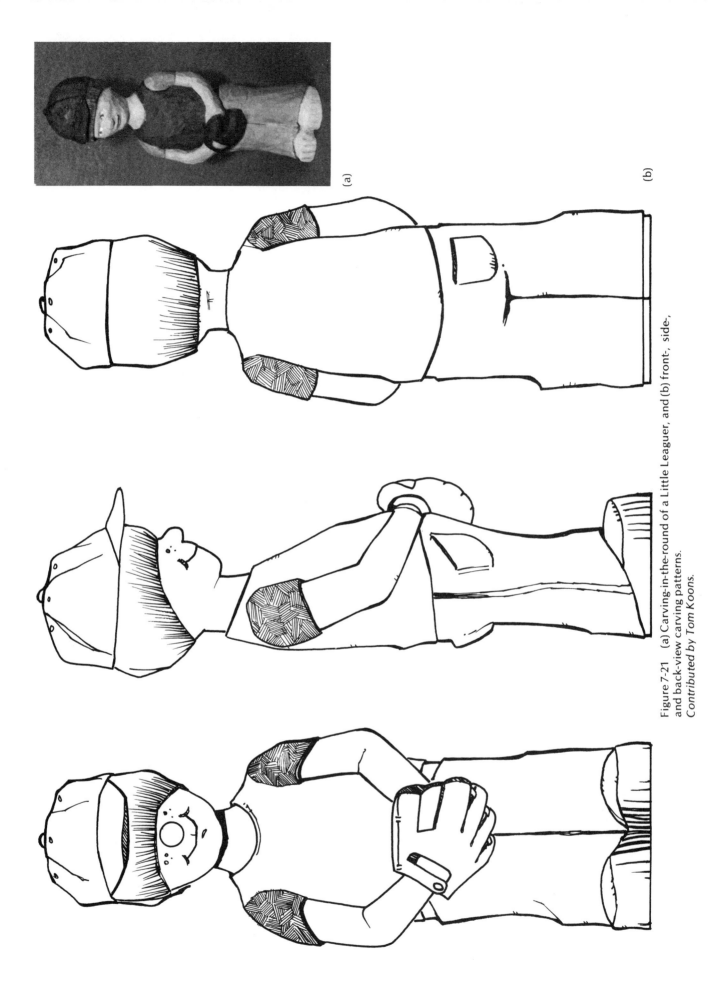

Figure 7-21 (a) Carving-in-the-round of a Little Leaguer, and (b) front, side, and back-view carving patterns. *Contributed by Tom Koons.*

Figure 7-22 (a) Carving-in-the-round of an elf, and (b) front-, side-, and back-view carving patterns. Contributed by Tom Koons.

87

(a)

(b)

Figure 7-23   (a) Carving-in-the-round of a mouse, and (b) front-, side-, and back-view carving patterns.

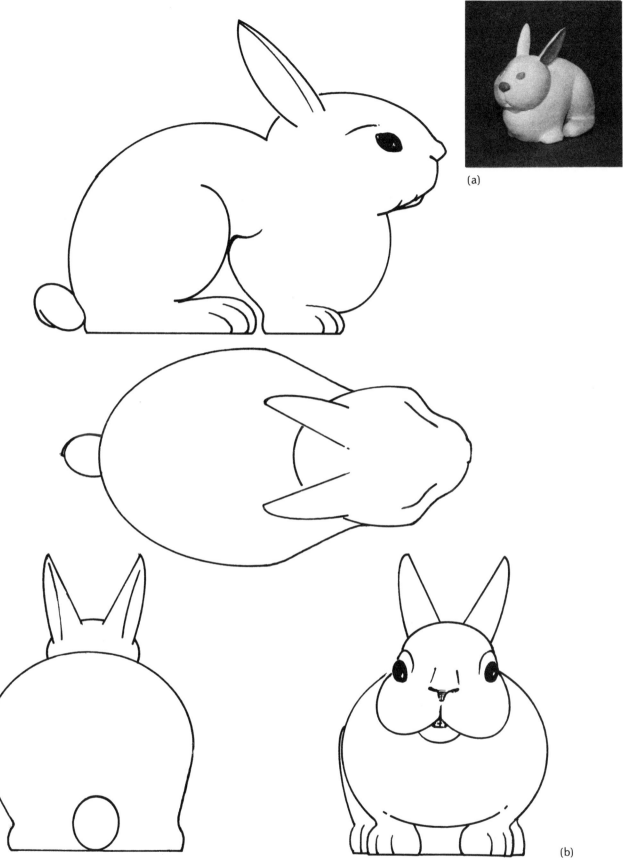

Figure 7-24   (a) Carving-in-the-round of a rabbit, and (b) side-, top-, back-, and front-view carving patterns.

89

(a)

(b)

Figure 7-25 (a) Carving-in-the-round of an owl, and (b) front-, back-, and side-view carving patterns.

Figure 7-26   (a) Carving-in-the-round of a hound, and (b) side-, front-, and top-view carving patterns.

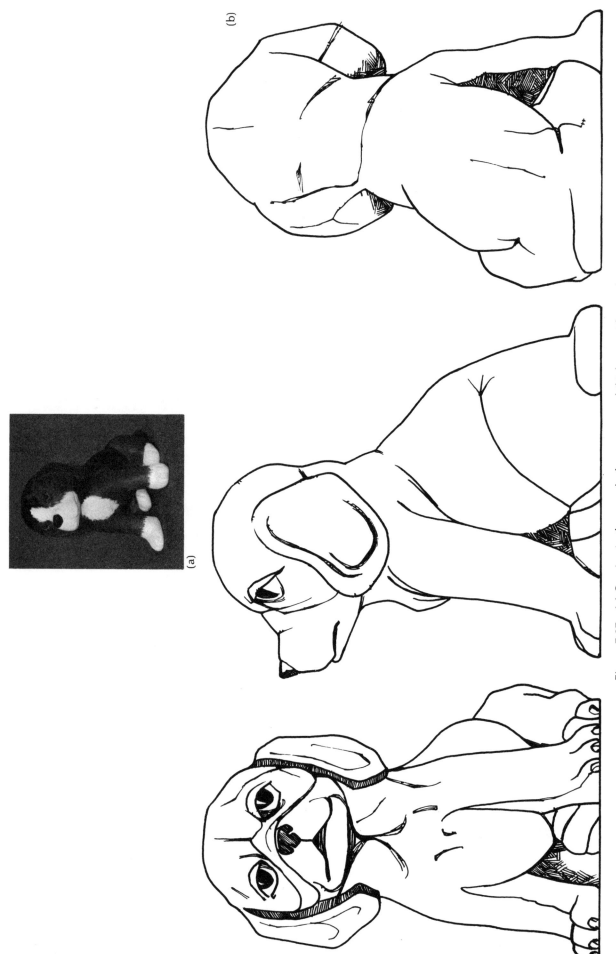

(b)

(a)

Figure 7-27 (a) Carving-in-the-round of a puppy, and (b) front-, side-, and back-view carving patterns.

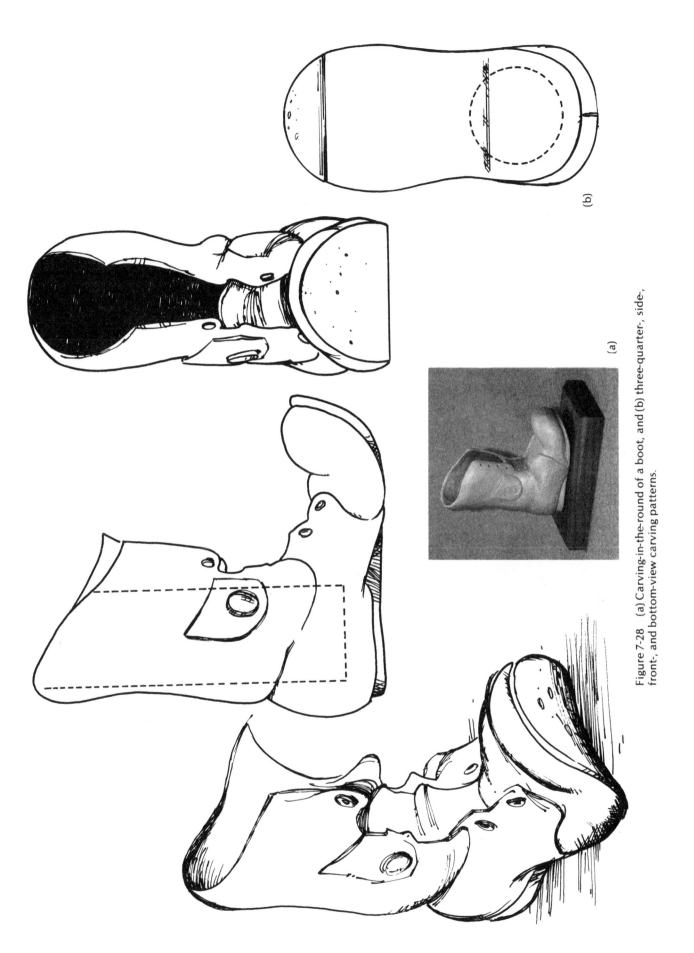

(b)

(a)

Figure 7-28 (a) Carving-in-the-round of a boot, and (b) three-quarter-, side-, front-, and bottom-view carving patterns.

Figure 7-29 Side- and top-view patterns for carving-in-the-round of a lion, with details of head and front paw.

Figure 7-30   Carving-in-the-round of Bucky Beaver.

Figure 7-31a   Front- and side-view patterns for carving-in-the-round of Bucky Beaver.

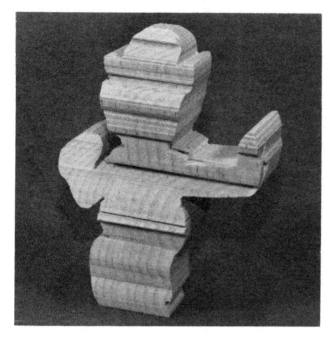

Figure 7-31b   Sawn out blank of Bucky Beaver.

Figure 7-31c   Arm sawed off.

Figure 7-31d   Arm.

Figure 7-31e   Arm in place.

Special note: After pattern is completely sawn out (7-31b),
saw off the arm (7-31c). Using a full 2-inch stock, saw out a
new arm through the full thickness of the 2-inch stock (7-
31d). Glue the new arm in the place of the one removed,
with the back of the arm lined up with the back of the pattern (7-31e); this is necessary so that you can place the hand
holding the toothpick out in front.

Figure 7-31f   Use these figures for examples of detail only. Do not try to saw out a blank from these views. Figure 7-31a gives the two-view pattern.

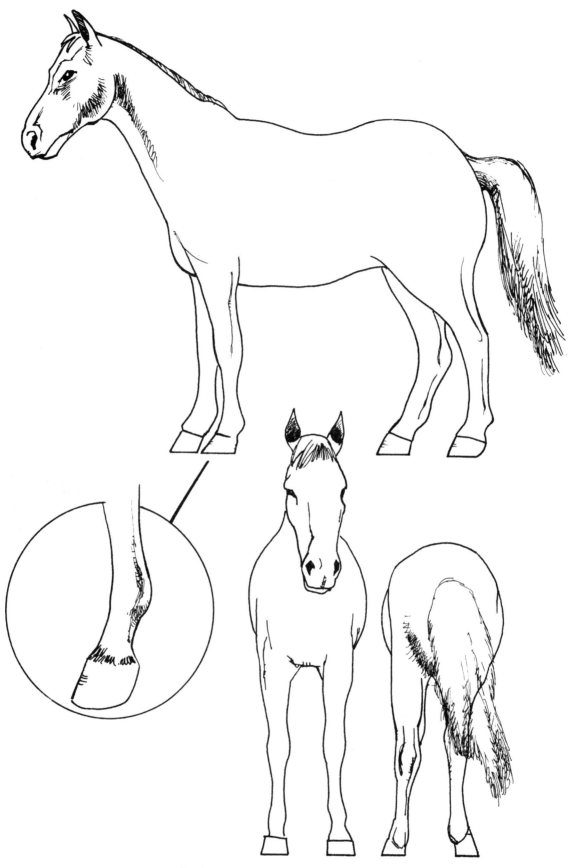

Figure 7-32   Side-, front-, and back-view patterns for carving-in-the-round of a horse, with detail of front left hoof.

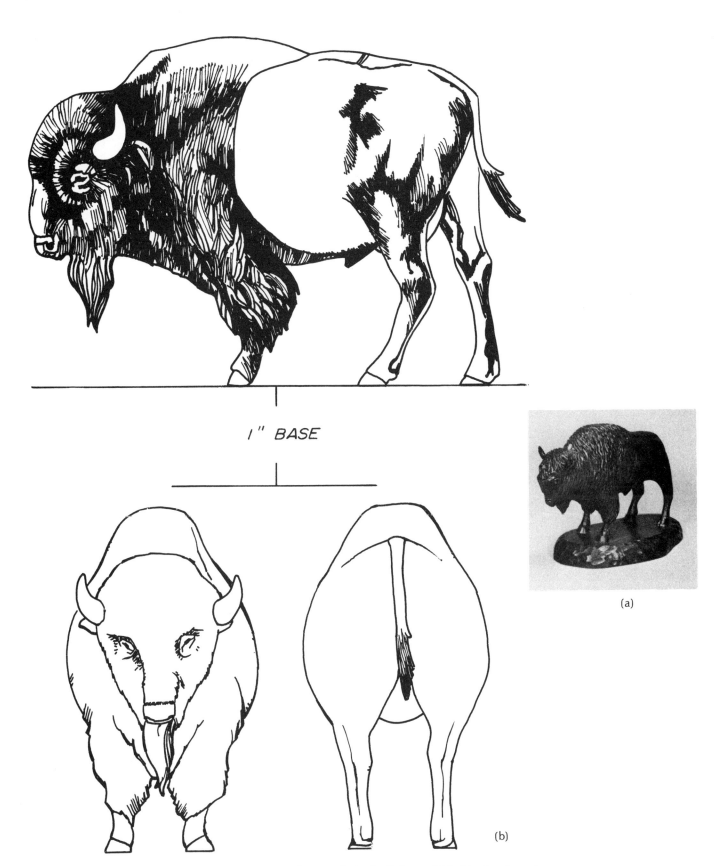

1" BASE

(a)

(b)

Figure 7-33 (a) Carving-in-the-round of a buffalo, and (b) side, front-, and back-view carving patterns.

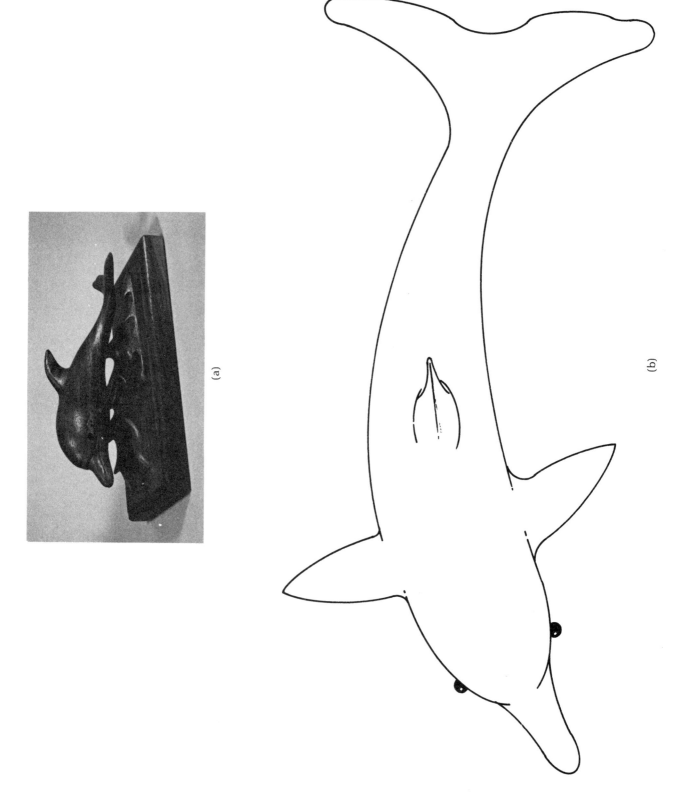

(a)

(b)

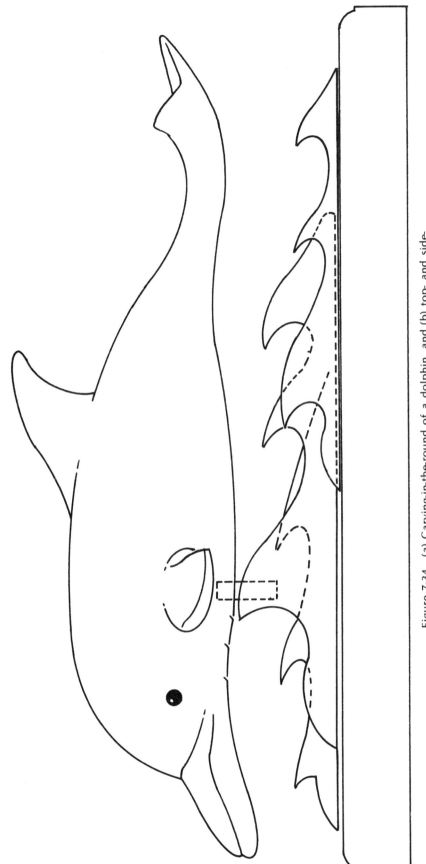

Figure 7-34 (a) Carving-in-the-round of a dolphin, and (b) top- and side-view carving patterns.

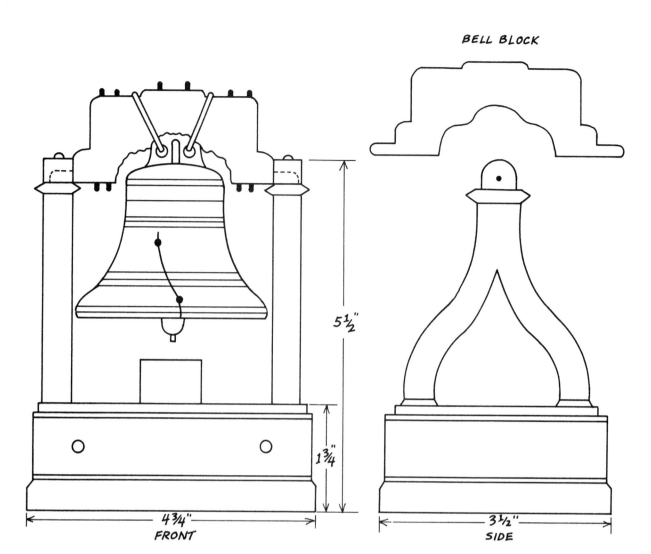

BELL BLOCK

5½"

1¾"

4¾"

FRONT

3½"

SIDE

(a)

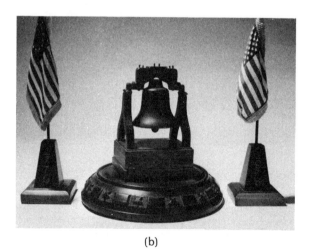

(b)

Figure 7-35   (a) Front- and side-view patterns for carving-in-the-round of the Liberty Bell (shown ⅔ actual size), and (b) carving-in-the-round of the Liberty Bell.

102

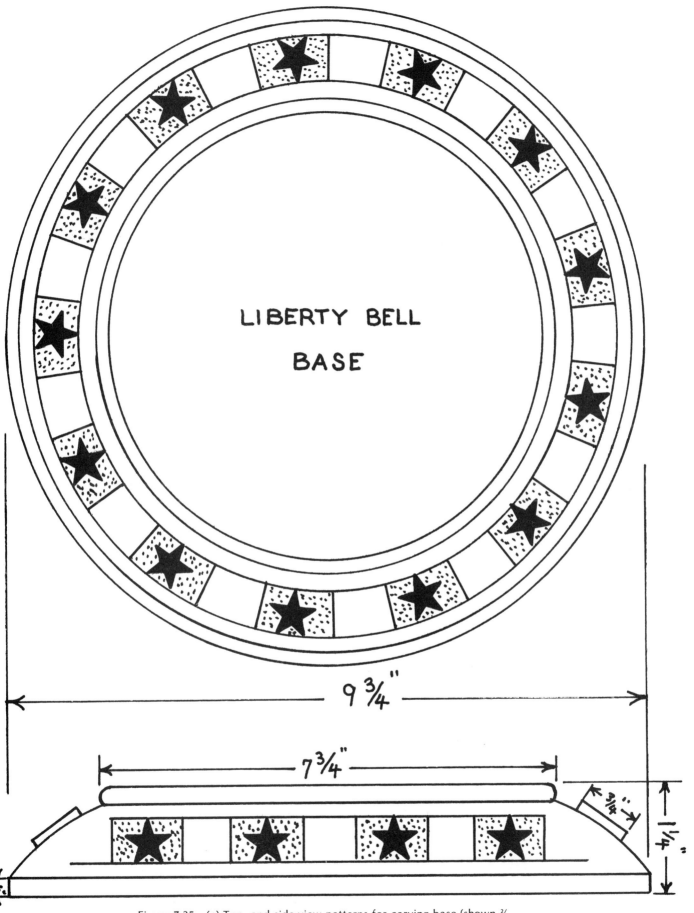

Figure 7-35 (c) Top- and side-view patterns for carving base (shown ⅔ actual size).

Figure 7-36 (a) Carving-in-the-round of Mr. and Mrs. Skunk, and (b) side-, front-, and back-view carving patterns. Insert your own inscription. Use your imagination!

(a)

(b)

(b)

Figure 7-37   (a) Carving-in-the-round of a mountain man, and (b) front- and
left-side carving patterns.

Figure 7-37   (c) Right- and back-view patterns for carving-in-the-round of a mountain man.

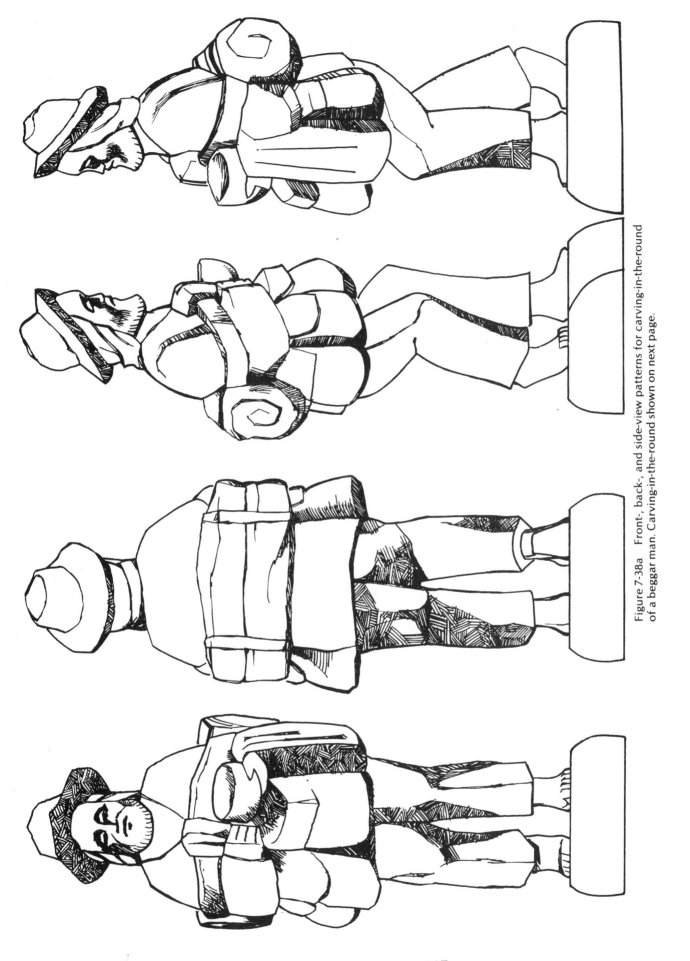

Figure 7-38a   Front-, back-, and side-view patterns for carving-in-the-round of a beggar man. Carving-in-the-round shown on next page.

107

Figure 7-38b   Carving-in-the-round of a beggar man.

8
Bird carving

One of the most appealing subjects for carvers is birds. Bird carving seems to dominate at most woodcarving shows. Exhibitions such as the world-famous shows sponsored by the Ward Foundation, The Louisiana Wildfowl Carving Guild, and the Wildfowl Festival of Easton, Maryland feature nothing but birds—waterfowl, shore birds, song birds, and birds of prey. In this chapter, we shall show you, step by step, how to carve a robin, discussing bird carving in general as we proceed.

Before you start

Since you will be painting your birds anyway, it is wise to start with either basswood or sugar pine, as these woods are easily carved and are relatively unsusceptible to splitting while you are doing detailwork. Always bear in mind that you want to carve with the grain as much as possible, so if your pattern calls for a tail that protrudes up or down, it is preferable to add a glued insert of wood with the grain running in that direction. You may even choose to carve the wings separately, attaching them to the body later to obtain an attitude of flight or landing.

Roughing out the bird

Transfer your pattern to your block of wood, being careful to line up the side and top views at the head and tail so that when they are cut out with the saw, they are not cut off.

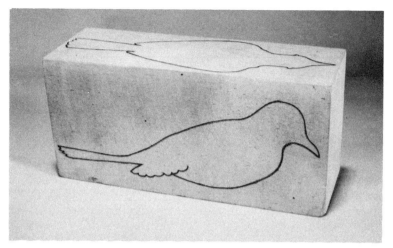

Figure 8-1   Step 1: Transfer your pattern to your block of wood.

With a band saw or hand coping saw, carefully cut around the outline, leaving 1/32 inch of wood to spare. Try to keep the bottom cut portion of the profile in one place because you will want to refasten it temporarily with a couple of brads in order to give you a flat working surface for your top-view cutting. Another method of accomplishing this is to bind all the pieces back together with ordinary masking tape to reform a complete block.

The resulting square block will be easier to handle and will place the top view in the correct position in relation to the side view.

While your block is still in rectangular form, drill a small hole straight through the head area so that you can position the eye accurately later on.

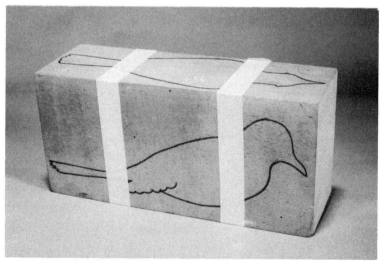

Figure 8-2   Step 2: Tape sawn-off pieces of the original block back in place.

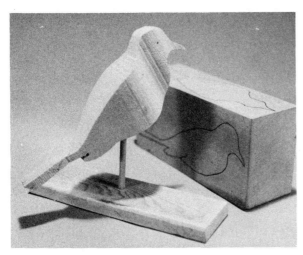

Figure 8-3   Sawn-out pattern.

After sawing out the top view, remove the tape, and you now have a perfect *blank* (a cut-out of the top and side contours of your subject) to start your carving.

Take the sawn block and rough out the rounded contours of the bird, referring to the drawings frequently. A Surform file or rasp may be used.

As you go, keep changing the area you are working on in order to give yourself a better perspective of the entire bird.

Now you are ready to begin the actual carving. Bear in mind that good carvers keep their tools razor-sharp at all times. This will ensure crisp, clean cuts. Be careful, as fingers also cut easily; always keep them clear of the cutting edge.

As you work, cut with the grain of the wood, turning the block in order to do so. Never work too long in one area, but rather carve different parts of the bird as you progress.

Figure 8-4   Step 3: Rough out the rounded contour of the bird. Step 4: Gradually shape the bird, continually changing the area you are working on.

111

Carving in the details

After you are satisfied that the bird has the final outline form you desire, begin cutting in the details with a sharp-pointed thin-bladed knife. Be very careful not to cut the feather detail too deep, since it is not natural in bird feather formations. Upon completing the feather formations, take a burning pen and score each feather to show detail. To avoid breakage, fragile areas, such as bills, wing tips, and tail feathers, should be the last items to be carved.

Upon completion of your carving you may choose to have your bird looking to the right or left. With a fine-toothed saw, such as a miter saw, carefully saw the head off just below the neck, then twist it slightly to the desired position and glue it in place. This will make a more lifelike piece and will enable you to create variations on the same bird pattern.

Figure 8-5 Step 5: Begin cutting in the details and burn in feathers.

Making birds' eyes

A variety of glass birds' eyes can be obtained from a good taxidermist's supply house, and be inserted into an oversized eye hole and bedded into epoxy putty, with a small edging of putty around the edge of the eye to form the eyelid and make it appear realistic.

BIRD EYES
Size in M/M and Color

Bird	Size	Color
Bittern	11	Yellow
Blackbird—Red Wing	5	Brown
Rusty	5	Brown
Brewers	6	Yellow
Yellow Headed	6	Brown
Blue Bird	4	Brown
Blue Jay	7	Hazel
Bobolink	5	Brown
Bob White Quail	8	Hazel
Bullfinch	6	Brown
Buzzard	12	Brown
Canary	3	Brown
Cardinal	5	Brown
Cat Bird	5	Brown
Chapparel Cock (Road Runner)	10	Yellow
Chickadee	4	Brown
Chicken—Domestic	10	Hazel
Coot	10	Red
Cormorant	8-12	Green
Cowbird	6	Brown
Crossbill	5	Brown
Crow	11	Brown
Cuckoo	7	Brown
Dove—Mourning	7	Brown
Turtle	7	Brown
White Winged	8	Orange
Duck—Bald Pate	10	Yellow
Black	11	Black
Buffle Head	10	Brown
Blue Bill	10	Yellow
Canvas Back	10	Red
Eider	11	Brown
Florida	11	Brown
Gadwall	11	Brown
Golden Eye	11	Yellow
Harlequin	10	Brown
Mallard	11	Brown
Merganser, American	11	Red
Merganser, Hooded	9	Yellow
Merganser, Red Br.	11	Yellow
Old Squaw	10	Hazel
Pintail	9	Brown
Red Head	10	Yellow
Ring Necked	10	Straw
Ruddy	11	Brown
Scaup	10	Yellow
Scoter	10	Yellow
Shoveller	10	Yellow
Spoon Bill	10	Yellow
Shell Drake	10	Red
Surf Scoter	10	White
Teal, Bluewing	9	Brown
Teal, Cinnamon	9	Yellow
Teal, Greenwing	9	Hazel
Whitewing Scoter	10	Straw
Widgeon	10	Yellow
Wood Duck	11	Red
Eagle—Bald Young	16	Brown
Bald Adult	17	Yellow
Golden	18	Brown
Falcon	12	Brown
Finches—Various	4	Brown
Flicker	8	Brown
Goose	12	Brown
Grackle	5	Straw
Grebe—Am. Eared	8	Red
Horned	9	Red
Pied Billed	8	Red
Grouse—Ruffed	10	Hazel
Gull—Black Backed	14	Yellow
Bonaparte	9	Brown
Franklin	9	Brown
Glaucus	14	Straw
Herring	12	Yellow
Laughing	10	Red
Ring Bill	10	Yellow
Hawk—Chicken	14	Hazel
Cooper	12	Straw
Fish (Osprey)	14	Yellow
Goshawk	14	Hazel
Hen	14	Hazel
Marsh	12	Yellow
Pigeon	8	Brown
Red Tail	14	Brown
Rough Leg	14	Hazel
Red Shoulder	14	Hazel
Sharp Shinned	10	Yellow
Sparrow	9	Brown
Swainsons	14	Hazel
Shoveler	10	Yellow
Kingfisher—Belted	10	Brown
Killdeer	7	Brown
Lark—Skylark	5	Brown
Loon	14	Red
Magpie	8	Brown
Meadowlark	7	Brown
Mocking Bird	5	Brown
Mudhen	10	Red
Nighthawk	8	Black
Osprey	14	Yellow
Owl—Arctic	20	Straw
Barn	14	Brown
Barred	18	Special
Burrowing	10	Yellow
Elf	10	Yellow

○ 2
○ 3
○ 4
○ 5
○ 6
7
8
9
10
11
12
13
14
15
16

Bird	Size	Color		Bird	Size	Color
Great Horned	20	Yellow		King	9	Brown
Long Eared	14	Yellow		Virginia	9	Hazel
Pigmy	12	Yellow		Yellow	6	Brown
Richardson	14	Yellow		Road Runner	10	Yellow
Screech	14	Straw		Robin	6	Brown
Sawwhet	12	Straw		Sandpiper	6 or 7	Brown
Snowy	18	Straw		Snipe	7	Brown
Short Eared	14	Yellow		Sparrow	3	Brown
Partridge	10	Hazel		Starling	5	Brown
Pelican	17	Straw		Swallow	4	Brown
Pheasant	10 or 11	Special		Tern	6	Brown
Pigeon	8	Orange		Thrush	6	Brown
Plover	6	Brown		Turkey—Wild	12	Brown
Prairie Chicken	10	Hazel		Woodpecker, Downy	5	Brown
Quail	8	Hazel		Flicker	8	Brown
Rails—Clapper	10	Hazel		Ivory Billed	12	Yellow
Carolina	8	Red		Red Bellied	7	Red
Little Black	5	Brown		Red Headed	6	Brown
				White Headed	6	Red

A very natural eye can also be produced in the following manner:

Cut 3 pieces of 1/8-inch dowel to about 3 inches in length. Take the first dowel and sand a very flat surface on the end. Gently dip this into a mixture of one-third white paint and two-thirds water, then very carefully touch the bird where you wish to place the eye. Hold it for a moment and then gently remove it.

Take the second dowel and carefully whittle it down smaller than the first. Dip this into a similar mixture of black paint and water and carefully place it on top of the white dot just a little high and off center.

Now take your third dowel and whittle it still smaller. Dip this into a mixture of brown paint and water and place a dot in the center of the black dot.

Now, with a very small paintbrush, place a tiny black dot in the center of the brown. Finally, with the tip of a straight pin dipped into white paint, place a tiny dot in the center of the black.

When the eyes are dry, coat them with high-gloss varnish, using a fine brush.

If these steps are followed very carefully, an eye will be produced that will look extremely natural.

The bird eye chart will prove useful in determining size and color. In ordering, purchase either clear or crystal eyes. By applying the correct color to the reverse surface of the eye, the desired effect will be obtained. Eyes are cheaper bought by the dozen. Painting your own will enable you to accommodate the various species, but do make sure that the size is correct.

Bear in mind that this chart is for full-size birds; if you are scaling your carving down in size, the eye size will have to be reduced proportionately. Most carvers have the tendency to use eyes that are too small. Do not be alarmed if the eye appears too large for your carving. Remember, it will be inserted into an oversized eye hole and bedded into epoxy putty, with a small edging of putty around the edge of the eye to form the eyelid and make it appear realistic.

Making birds' legs

Many good bird carvers spoil a good bird carving by giving the legs an undesirable "pipe stem" effect by using a couple of old nails as legs.

If you were to look at Aunt Matilda's pet canary, you would note that the bird's legs are not round, but are flat on the sides with a rounded radius on the front and a smaller rounded radius on the back. This effect can be achieved by pounding the sides of a small finishing nail of the proper size after the leg is bent for the knee joint. Epoxy glue can be used to build up the thicker areas of the leg.

For a more naturalistic stance, position one leg at a slightly more forward angle than the other. This will be determined by the type of mounting you choose.

Epoxy or water putty can be shaped where the leg joins the body to achieve a more naturalistic contour with the body.

Making birds' feet

There are, of course, many clever methods of making birds' feet. The method we think is most authentic is to take a piece of heavy-gauge aluminum and file angular cuts in from the edge of the metal in the shape of a medium V. Now file

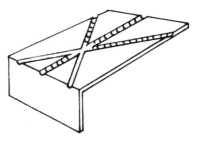

Figure 8-6 Bird's foot mold.

another cut straight up from the middle of the *V*, making it a little longer than the previous cuts.

To add a touch of realism to the upper side of the feet it is necessary to provide cross ridges on each toe. To gain this effect, take a small round piece of steel stock and fashion it into a small chisel with a rounded end. Carefully make a

Figure 8-7   Making birds' feet from hammered lead.

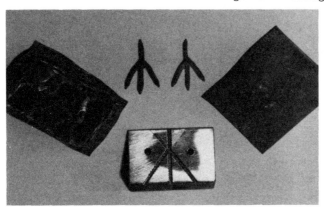

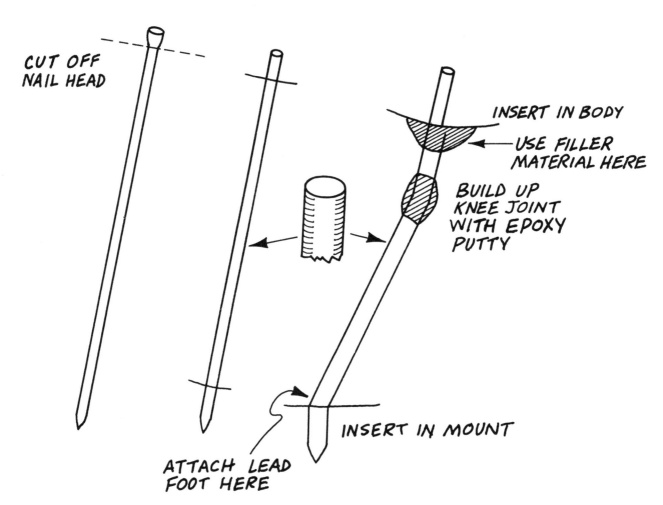

CUT OFF NAIL HEAD

INSERT IN BODY

USE FILLER MATERIAL HERE

BUILD UP KNEE JOINT WITH EPOXY PUTTY

ATTACH LEAD FOOT HERE

INSERT IN MOUNT

series of indentations up each toe of your aluminum mold. If this is done carefully, a very satisfactory realistic foot will be produced. This will give you a mold from which to fashion the feet.

Obtain a sheet of lead from your local plumber. Place this over your mold and hammer it until it is paper-thin. When you remove it from the mold, you will have a perfect imprint of a foot with a web between the toes. With a small pair of scissors, carefully clip the excess material out from between the toes and carefully trim the remaining toes to shape. Bend the tips just a little to form claws.

Painting the bird

You are now ready to paint your carving. Follow the instructions as set forth in the next chapter. For correct shades of colors when painting, refer to the color pictures in bird books available from your local library and the pictures you have clipped for your reference file. And remember, *take your time. Nothing was ever done right in a hurry!*

Figure 8-8   Step 6: Mount and paint the finished bird.

Mounting the bird

To display your bird to its best possible advantage, some care should be taken in the choice of a mount. Since birds are wild creatures, a natural mount is advised. You may wish him perched on the tip of a branch or perhaps on a slab of wood with the bark still attached. A piece of white birch is quite effective in many cases. A walk along a stream or riverbank will reward you with a wide selection of driftwood. Pieces of gnarled wood or roots bleached in the sun also serve well. Do not use green wood since it tends to split as it dries.

To attach your bird to its mount, drill a hole in the branch or slab where you wish to position each foot, anchoring each leg with epoxy glue. Let dry overnight in a warm place. Now attach the lead foot, forming the toes around the branch or on the base in the desired position, and anchor with a good glue. Touch up the feet and legs with a fine brush and acrylic paint.

Should you desire to carve a flying bird, it may be suspended by a nylon thread or be made into a mobile of several birds.

Another method of mounting might be to take a stiff wire and curve it into a graceful arc, then embed the top into the belly of the bird and the bottom into the base.

If you follow the instructions given, you should be able to produce a carving of which you will be proud. The following collection of patterns have been provided for your enjoyment and to give you a variety of choice.

(a)

(b)

Figure 8-9   Ideas for mounts for bird carvings.

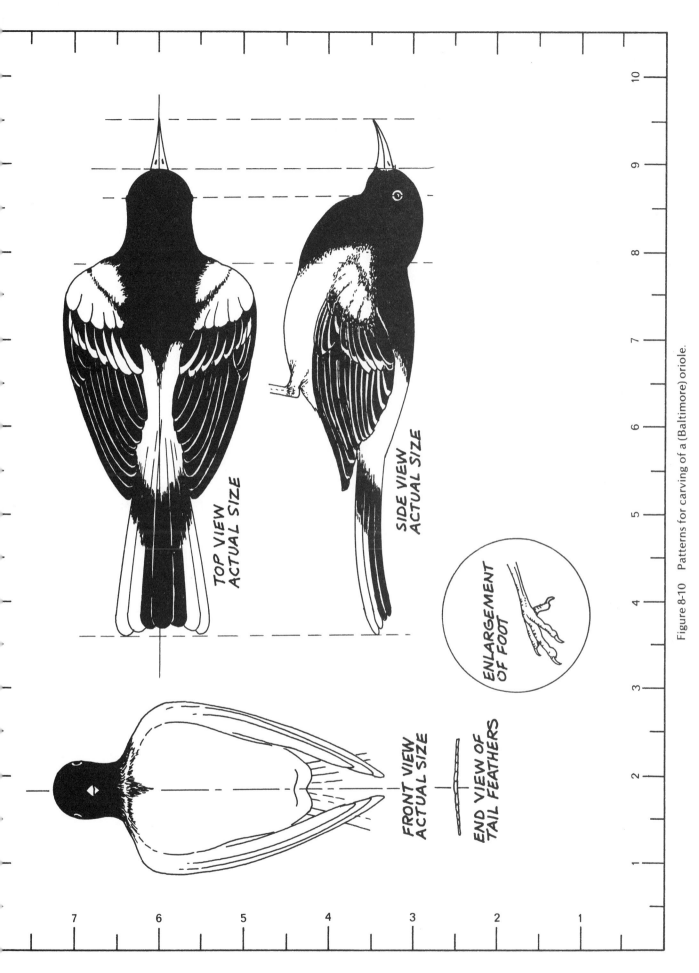

TOP VIEW
ACTUAL SIZE

SIDE VIEW
ACTUAL SIZE

ENLARGEMENT
OF FOOT

FRONT VIEW
ACTUAL SIZE

END VIEW OF
TAIL FEATHERS

Figure 8-10   Patterns for carving of a (Baltimore) oriole.

119

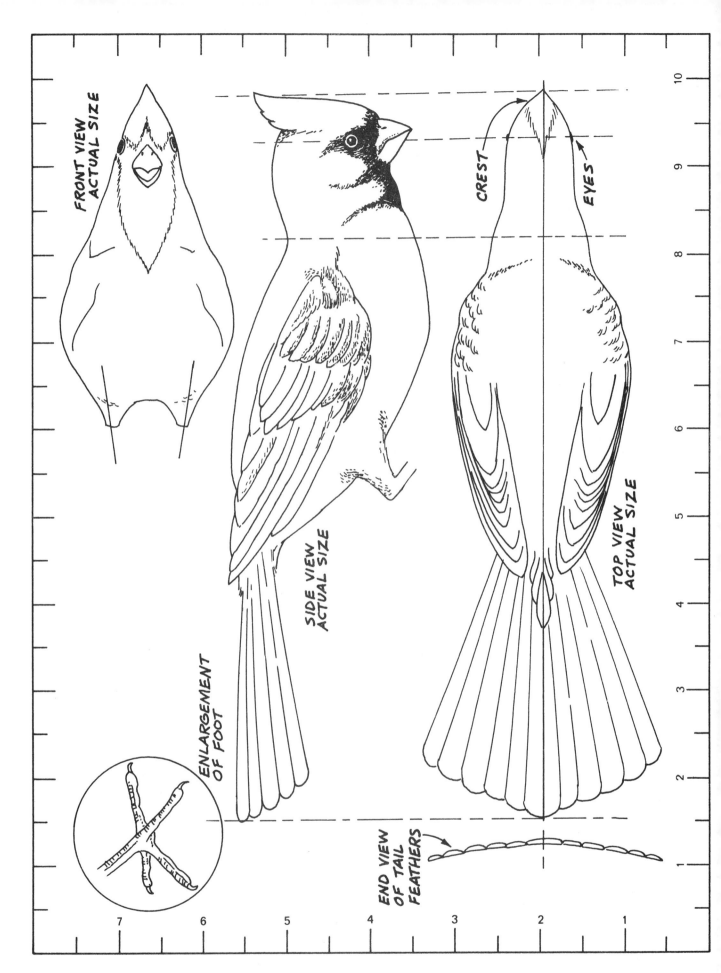

FRONT VIEW
ACTUAL SIZE

SIDE VIEW
ACTUAL SIZE

TOP VIEW
ACTUAL SIZE

CREST

EYES

ENLARGEMENT
OF FOOT

END VIEW
OF TAIL
FEATHERS

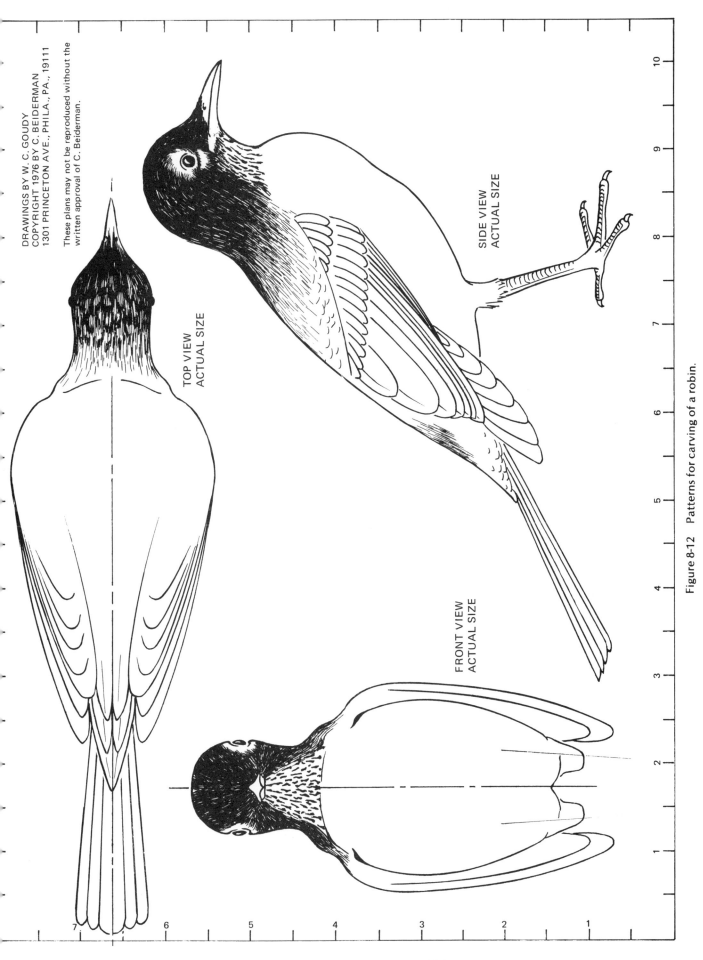

TOP VIEW
ACTUAL SIZE

SIDE VIEW
ACTUAL SIZE

FRONT VIEW
ACTUAL SIZE

Figure 8-12   Patterns for carving of a robin.

121

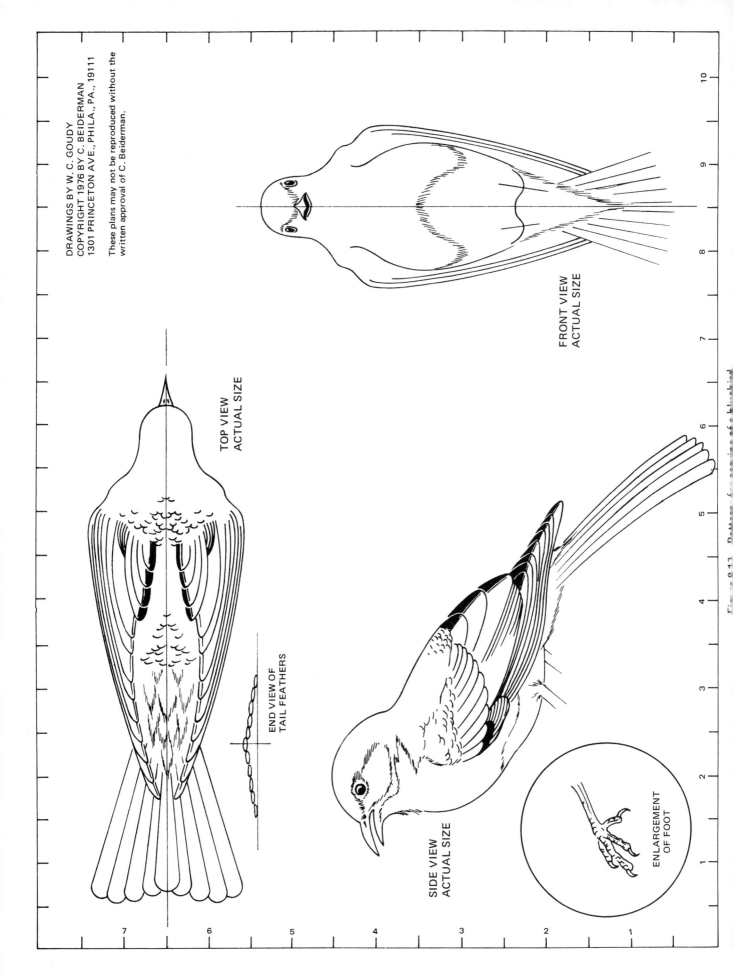

TOP VIEW
ACTUAL SIZE

END VIEW OF
TAIL FEATHERS

FRONT VIEW
ACTUAL SIZE

SIDE VIEW
ACTUAL SIZE

ENLARGEMENT
OF FOOT

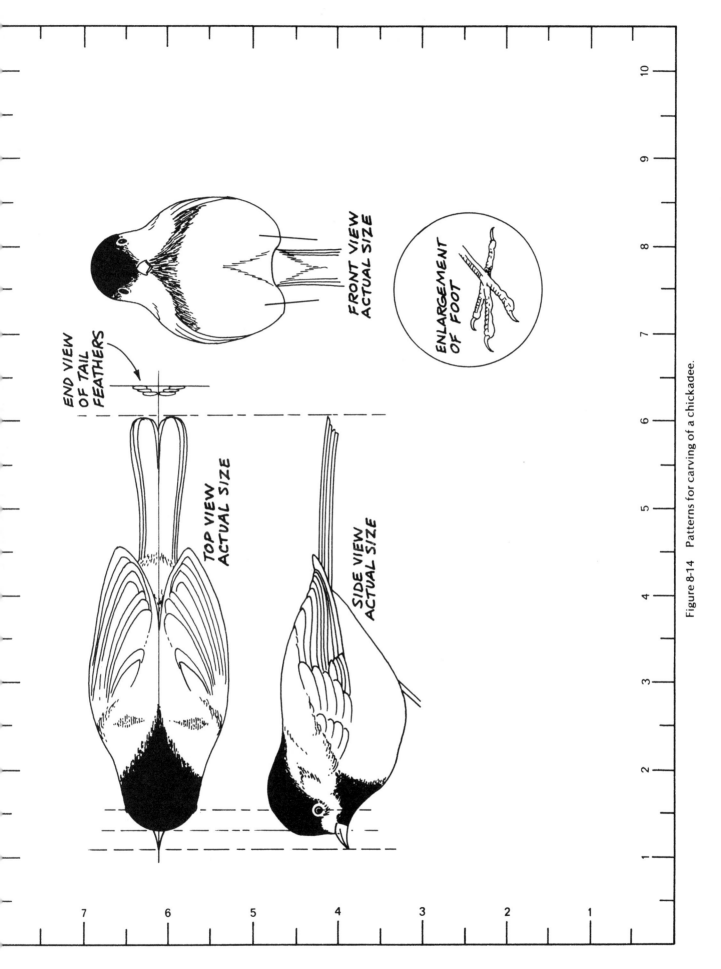

END VIEW
OF TAIL
FEATHERS

FRONT VIEW
ACTUAL SIZE

ENLARGEMENT
OF FOOT

TOP VIEW
ACTUAL SIZE

SIDE VIEW
ACTUAL SIZE

Figure 8-14 Patterns for carving of a chickadee.

123

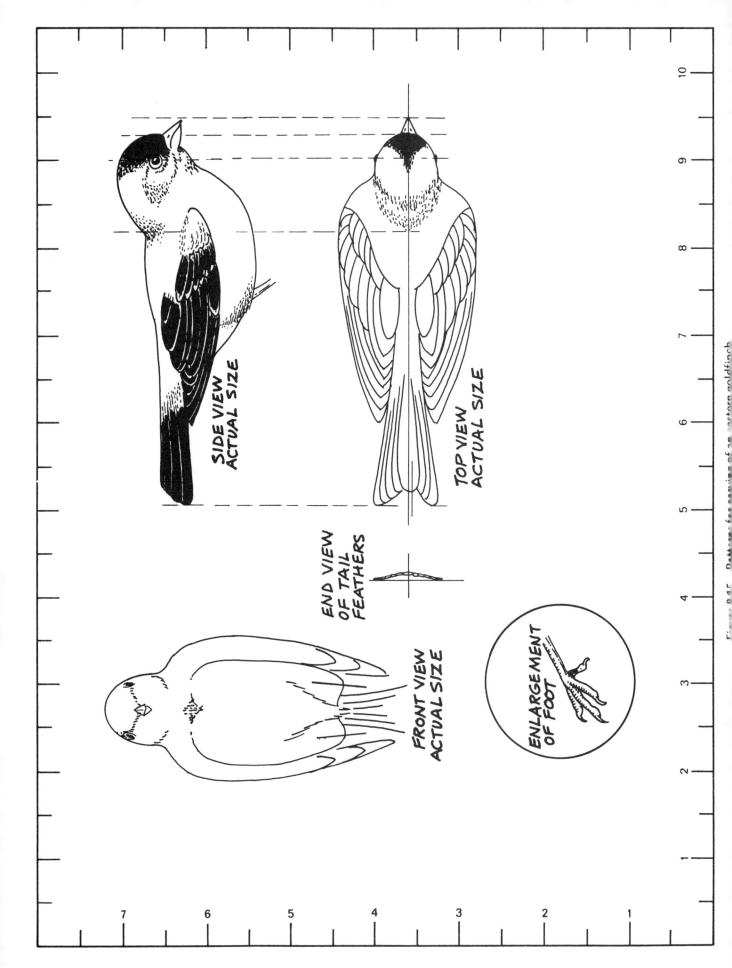

SIDE VIEW
ACTUAL SIZE

TOP VIEW
ACTUAL SIZE

END VIEW
OF TAIL
FEATHERS

FRONT VIEW
ACTUAL SIZE

ENLARGEMENT
OF FOOT

Figure 9.15 — Pattern for carving of an eastern goldfinch.

124

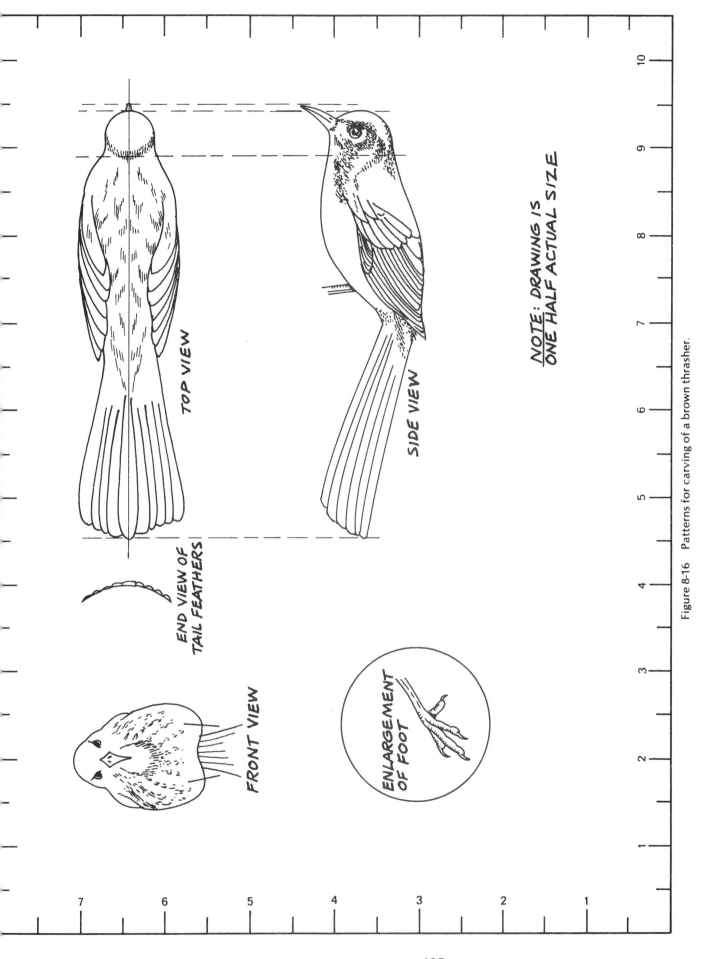

TOP VIEW

SIDE VIEW

END VIEW OF TAIL FEATHERS

FRONT VIEW

ENLARGEMENT OF FOOT

<u>NOTE</u>: DRAWING IS ONE HALF ACTUAL SIZE

Figure 8-16   Patterns for carving of a brown thrasher.

125

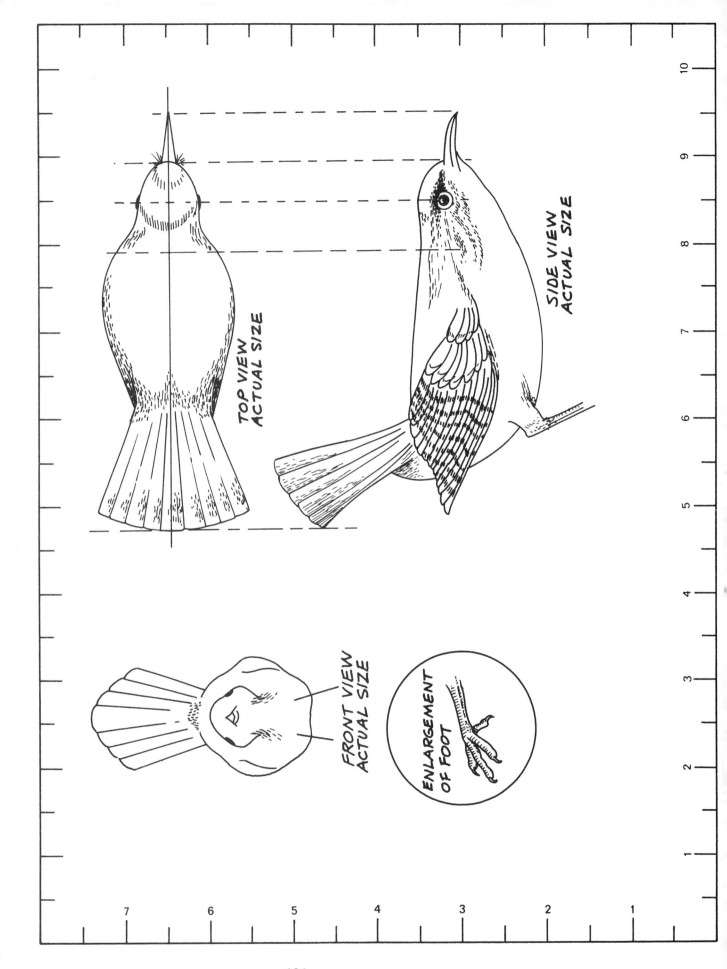

TOP VIEW
ACTUAL SIZE

SIDE VIEW
ACTUAL SIZE

FRONT VIEW
ACTUAL SIZE

ENLARGEMENT
OF FOOT

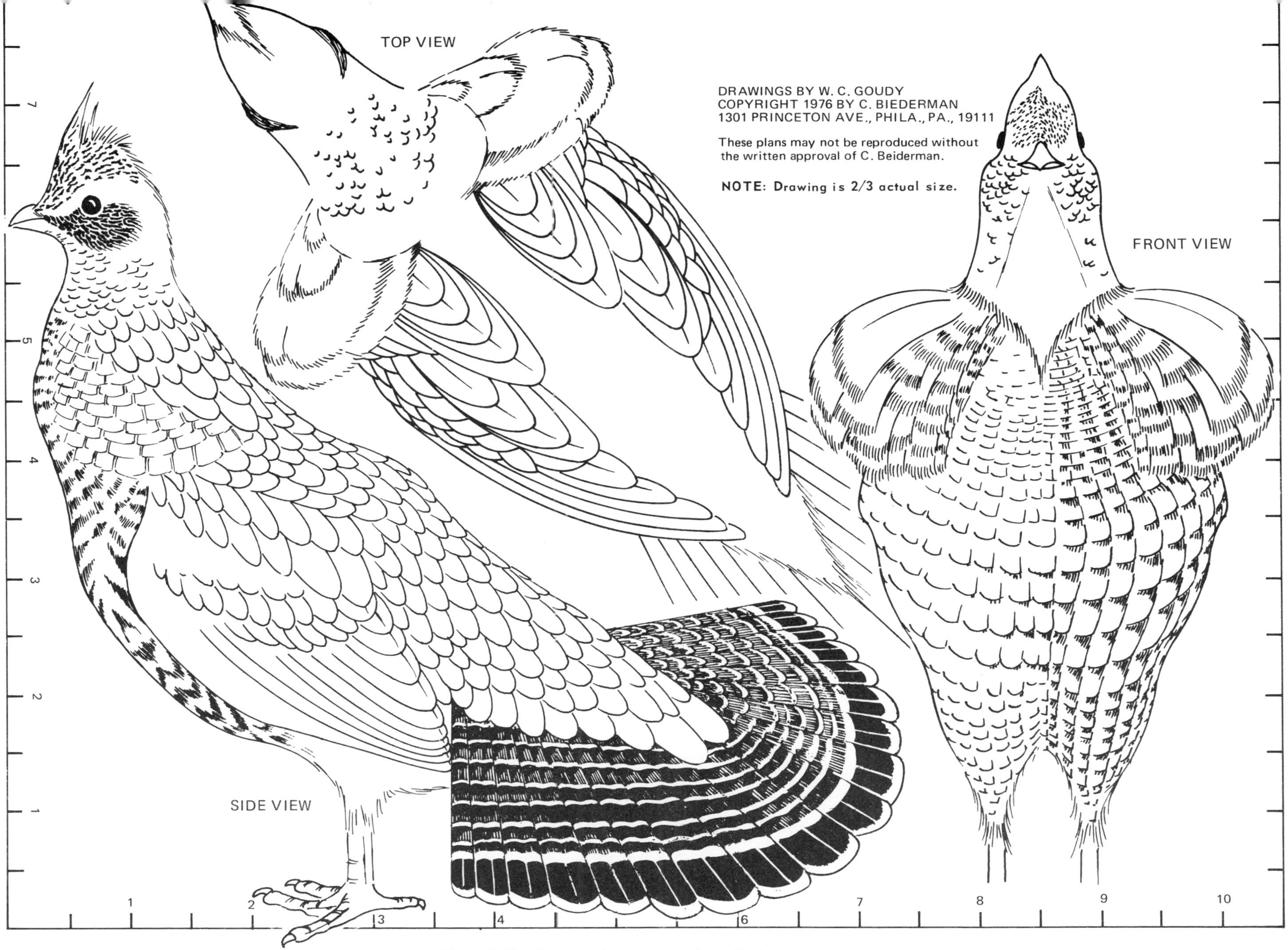

FRONT VIEW

TOP VIEW

SIDE VIEW

Figure 8-18   Patterns for carving of a ruffed grouse.

9

Painting and finishing

Upon completion of your carving you will be faced with the decision of what kind of finish you will want to apply. The factors in your decision will be the variety of wood you have used and the carving you have made. Woods with unattractive grains such as basswood and sugar pine are better painted. Refer to the wood reference chart in Chapter 2 for finishing characteristics of the various woods.

Staining, waxing, or varnishing your woodcarving

If the wood you have used is one of those with a beautiful grain pattern, such as walnut, mahogany, or one of the fruitwoods, a natural finish with a light stain or just the application of a satin varnish or paste wax will enhance the natural beauty of the wood. Shoe polish buffed to a sheen may also give that glowing, soft effect you have been seeking. Always try the finish on a piece of scrap wood of the same type as your carving first. Remember, once you have applied wax or shoe polish, you will not be able to paint or varnish it—that will be it!

In applying stain, follow the directions on the can. Keep in mind that the longer a stain sets before being rubbed with a cloth, the darker it will be. Remember, too, that wood darkens with age naturally, so don't make your stain too dark. The end grain of the wood will usually stain darker; to overcome this, apply a coat of equal parts shellac and alcohol to act as a partial sealer before applying the stain.

There are several ways to stain wood besides using commercial stain. Strong tea will impart a pleasing stain. An old trick to turn wood a silvery gray involves steeping rusty nails in vinegar overnight, then applying the solution with smooth brushstrokes.

Liquid dye that is used for fabrics can also produce pleasant results in staining wood. The dye imparts a color as faint or as intense as you want, yet allows the beauty of the natural grain to show through. Interesting, too, are the range of colors available—some thirty-five to choose from plus whatever you can obtain by doing your own mixing.

Should you decide on a varnish finish, by all means choose a satin or eggshell finish. It will impart a soft sheen that will let the natural beauty of the wood be appreciated. A high-gloss varnish is fine for the transom and woodwork of a cabin cruiser but is a bit garish for woodcarvings—it's like the difference between neon light and candlelight!

Painting your woodcarving

If your carving is to be painted, you have the choice of using either acrylic paints or oils. Both have advantages and disadvantages.

Since oils do not dry rapidly, it is easy to blend colors; however, they take such a long time to dry that you must often let one color dry overnight before working on another.

Acrylics, on the other hand, dry very rapidly, too fast in many cases. This can be controlled somewhat by the addition of a retarder, which slows down the drying process. With acrylics you can work from one color to another in a matter of minutes, which is why many carvers and artists have switched to this water-based paint. Any inexpensive book on painting with acrylics that is available at art stores will help you in mastering the technique of this medium.

Acrylic paints are our preference, so the tips that follow will apply to this type of paint. Good brushes are essential; sable are to be preferred. Three or four flats and the same number of rounds should see you well on your way.

When you are satisfied that your carving is finished and is ready for painting, give it a light sanding, and, as a sealer, apply a coat of gesso or outside white latex paint, which works just as well. When thoroughly dry, sand lightly with fine paper again.

When you paint, handle your subject as little as possible, because the oils from your hands will prevent good adhesion of the acrylic paint. Always wash your hands prior to painting. In fact, an excellent tip is to attach your holding stick to the bottom of the carving and hold it with that, or clamp the holding stick in your vise, thus freeing both hands.

Another tip when working with acrylics is to fill with water one of those plastic squeeze bottles that hair conditioners come in; the spout will enable you to squeeze out either a single drop or healthy squirt, whichever you need, when mixing paint.

In the instructions that follow, you will note that we have made repeated reference to the painting of bird carvings. This has been intentional, our reasoning being that if you are able to master the blending of colors in a bird's plumage, you will have litte trouble painting any other type of carving.

So, if your subject is a bird, sketch over the carving of the feathering with a pencil to provide a guide in painting. Should you wish your carving to look particularly realistic, this is the time to put your burning pen to work. After burning, go over the carving with fine steel wool, follow with a thorough brushing or vacuuming, and you are ready for the final painting.

The wash method is superior in painting burned feather detail, because a thick coat of paint would obscure the fine detail you have painstakingly strived to achieve. Since acrylic paints dry rapidly, make it a practice when painting a bird to paint three or four feathers on one wing, then switch over and paint the corresponding feathers on the opposite wing. This way if you have to mix up more paint, you won't wind up with one wing painted with one shade and the other wing painted with another shade in the event that you can't get the two paint mixtures exactly alike. (And we never can!)

In painting birds, paint the dark markings, such as the bars on a blue jay's feathers, first. When these markings are dry, mix up a wash—that is, a watery mix of color—and apply it with a wide brush. This will impart a tint. And since these paints dry almost instantly, you can apply repeated coats within a short period of time. The use of a hot-air hair drier will speed this process up even more rapidly. Each successive coat will deposit a little more color; just continue the washes until you have reached the desired hue.

A set of five tubes of iridescent acrylic paints can be purchased at an art supply store and will prove very useful in capturing a realistic effect in birds. Made of very finely ground mica flakes, they can be blended in with colors very easily. A word of warning, though: Use very sparingly or your carving will look like one of those "Made in Hong Kong" tinseled prizes you win at a shooting gallery! Try just a touch of iridescent gold on the cheeks and in a line down the middle of the sides of the neck of the next mallard you paint, and blend it in with dark green. With a little practice, the results will astound you.

Special effects, such as vermiculation in waterfowl, can be applied with an architect's pen using India ink. Although this is sold as waterproof ink, it is not entirely so; it will run or rub off unless you spray a coat of clear satin lacquer over it. As an alternative, black acrylic paint may be applied with a fine pen nib inserted in a wooden pen holder.

If you use a spraypaint, always coat the glass eyes of your bird with a liquid masking, available at art supply shops. This will protect them, and they will be bright and clear upon removal of the masking at the completion of the painting process.

Remember that carvings often have been spoiled by poor painting. Our efforts should be directed toward having the painting and finishing enhance the carving in a light, soft manner. The techniques of painting and finishing are skills that must be mastered like anything else. But once having mastered them, the carver is assured of a beautiful piece of work.

10
Woodcarvings as gifts

By the time you have reached this chapter of the book, the mantel over your fireplace and the bookshelves in your home should be heavily laden with your carvings. It is time now to think of how your skill can be put to functional use. Just think, never again will you have to wonder what to give for birthday, Christmas, or wedding gifts. All you will need is a little time and your newly acquired skills as a woodcarver!

Figure 10-1   Wooden boxes decorated by various carving techniques.

The following list should provide you with plenty of ideas:

- A carver's design in relief will enhance picture frames, jewelry boxes, plaques, trays, and many similar items.

Figure 10-2   Miniature bird carvings mounted on desk pen holders.

- A relief carving of a person's dog or pet is always a welcome gift.

- Songbirds can be mounted onto a piece of gnarled branch to become an unusual wall hanging.

- Small carved whales, fish, and seabirds attached to bits of driftwood make attractive mobiles.

- Miniature figures and waterfowl mounted on a base make nice desk pen holders. Pens for this purpose with swivel mounts are available from specialty wood supply houses. If you want to go all out, have the recipient's name engraved on a brass plate and attach it to the base. Glue green felt onto the base bottom, and you have a gift of distinction!

- Carve a full-sized mallard or wood duck, make it into a table lamp, and top it off with a burlap shade. Just the thing for a boy's room or a sportsman's den, it will be enjoyed for years.

- Many patterns are obtainable for pull toys and action toys that will delight children.

Figure 10-3   Duck carving made into a table lamp.

134

- Three-dimensional puzzles are fun to make and will be well received by people of all ages.

- If you have a young friend who is active in Scouting, carve him a series of neckerchief slides—they will be the envy of the troop!

- A hand-carved cane can become a cherished possession. It is a custom among carvers to collaborate on a "friendship cane." You select a stout piece of wood (preferably a hardwood) and carve the handle. It then gets passed on to a carving friend, who adds a carving before passing it on to another carver. Once it has made the rounds and is completely carved, it comes back to you—a beautiful conversation piece and a memento of all your carving friends.

Figure 10-4   Friendship canes.

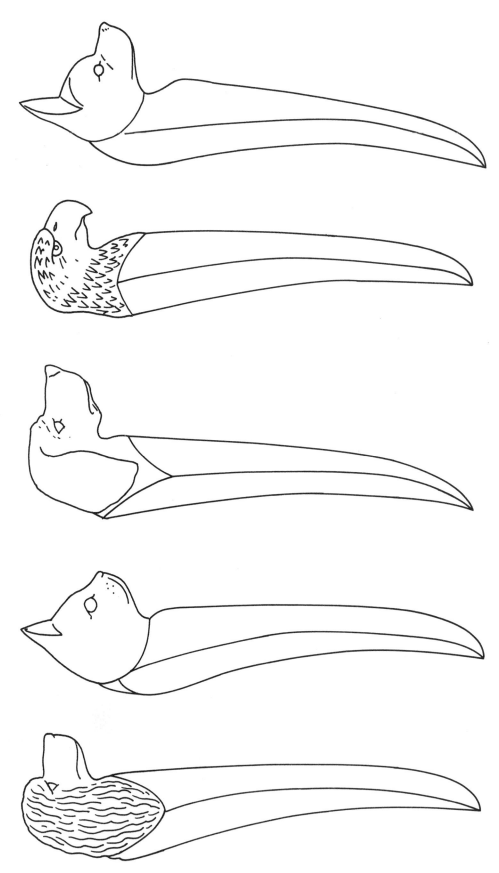

Figure 10-5a

- If you have any friends with an ethnic background, perhaps you would like to carve them plaques with their ancestral country's emblem or national flag or perhaps their family coat of arms or crest.

- A hand-carved sign for a friend who has a place of business would be gratefully received.

- A special hand-carved shoe horn (shown in Fig. 10-7) would make a splendid gift for a special event or for Christmas. Very interesting effects can be attained by combining unusual woods in their construction, giving them individuality. A variety of effects in the handles can be attained by preparing a glued-up block of several species of wood as shown in Figure 10-8. We have included a special set of patterns for your convenience and step-by-step directions to help you in completing one or more of the projects.

As your work becomes known, you will find that people will seek you out to purchase your carvings for unusual gifts for those special people on their list.

The wonderful thing about a carving gift is that you are not just giving a gift, you are giving of yourself—your skill and your patience, which are things that cannot be bought in a gift shop. It will be a gift that will bring back fond memories of your friendship and will be cherished and treasured as the years go by.

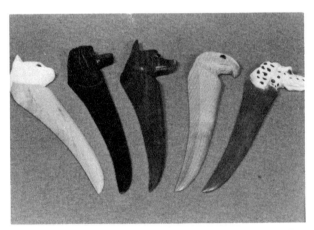

Figure 10-5b   A collection of letter openers carved by Allen Kerr, of Lancaster, Pa. They are reproduced with the permission of his widow, Dorothy M. Kerr.

Figure 10-6   Shoe horns.

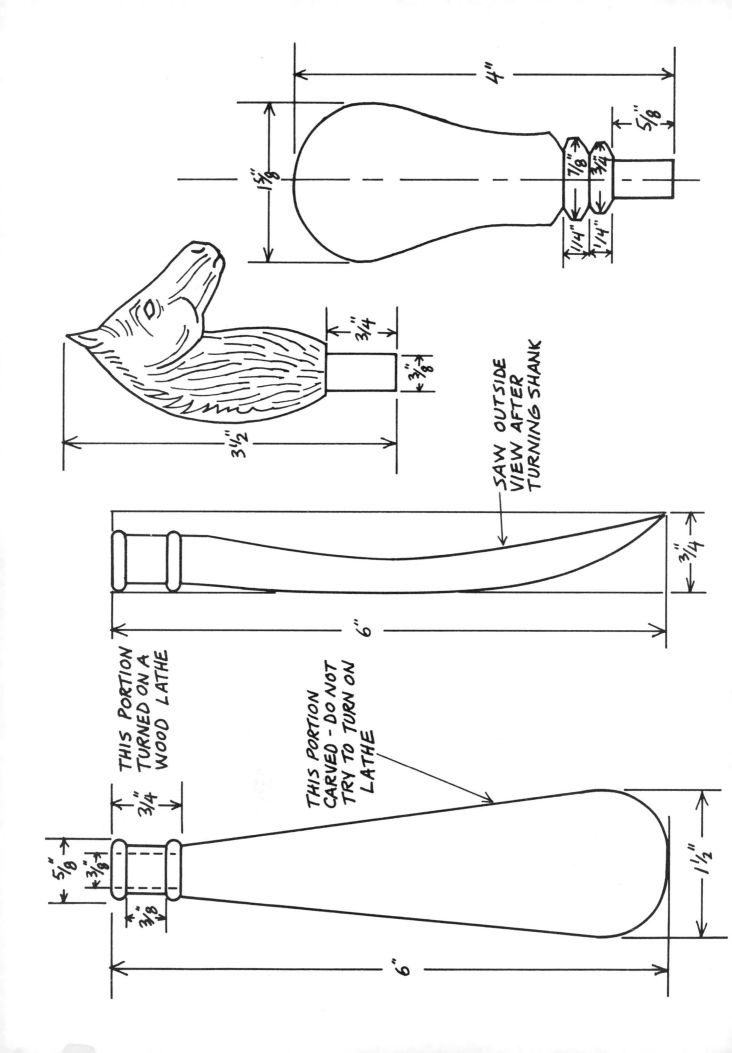

4"

1⅝"

7/8" 3/4"

1/4" 1/4"

5/8"

3/4"

3/8"

3½"

SAW OUTSIDE VIEW AFTER TURNING SHANK

3/4"

6"

THIS PORTION TURNED ON A WOOD LATHE

THIS PORTION CARVED - DO NOT TRY TO TURN ON LATHE

5/8"

3/8"

3/8"

3/4"

1½"

6"

Figure 10-7b   Shoe horns.

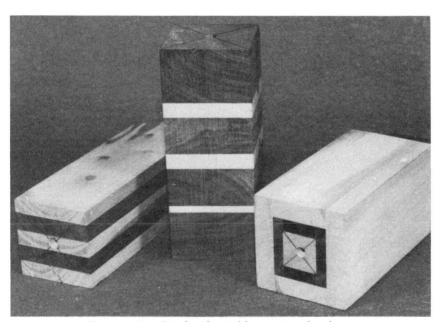

Figure 10-7c   Blocks of wood for carving shoe horns.

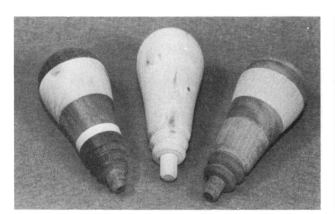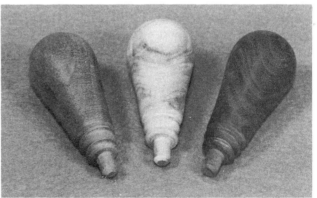

Figure 10-7d & e   The handles shown were fashioned from such woods as walnut, holly, mimosa, cherry, butternut, and maple. Patterns follow on next page.

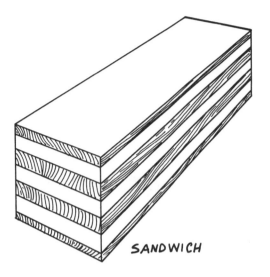

SANDWICH

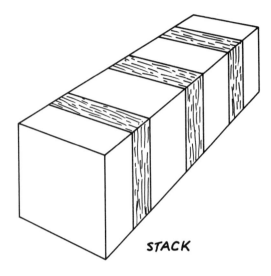

STACK

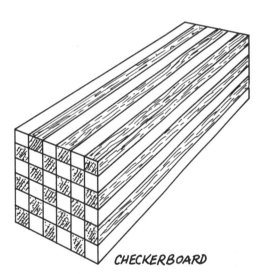

CHECKERBOARD

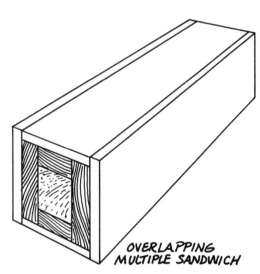

OVERLAPPING
MULTIPLE SANDWICH

Figure 10-7f Sandwich Pattern: Simply glue up alternating strips of contrasting woods. Stack: Glue up a stack of various contrasting woods to a length needed to turn a full handle. Checkerboard: Cut a number of equal side strips of contrasting woods and glue them alternately into a checkerboard pattern. Multiple Sandwich: Glue up carefully squared strips and blocks starting with an equal square as the core.

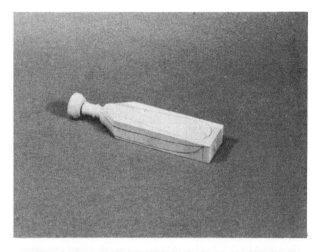

Figure 10-8a   Step 1: Cut a block 7½″ × 2″ × ¾″ from any type of hardwood. Center it in a lathe and turn the upper part of the blade. When turning is completed, trace the top and side views to the block. (It is a good idea to make a cardboard template of each view and trace around it.)

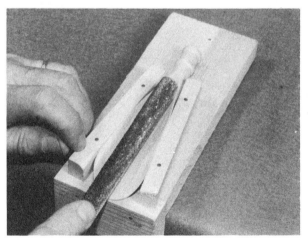

Figure 10-8b   Step 2: Band-saw out both views of the blade.

Figure 10-8c   Step 3: From scrap wood fashion a holding jig for the blade blank. With a gouge carve out the inside curve of the blade. (Be certain to carve the outside curve of the blank as well.)

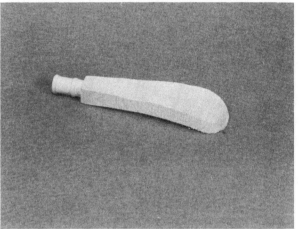

Figure 10-8d   Step 4: Fashion another holding jig and rough-sand the inside of the blade by fastening a rough grade of paper to a dowel stick.

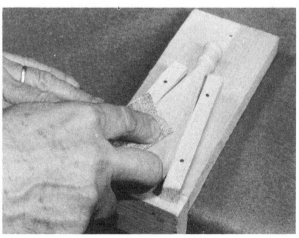

Figure 10-8e   Step 5: Finish sanding with finer grades of paper until a satisfactory finish is obtained.

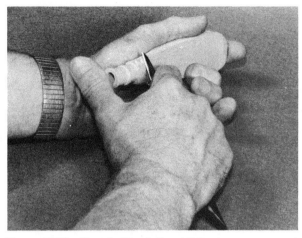

Figure 10-8f   Step 6: Carefully whittle the area around the turned portion of the blade with your knife. This is done to prevent the rotary rasp shown in Step 7 from damaging the turning.

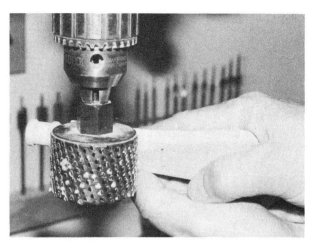

Figure 10-8g   Step 7: Roughly form the back of the blade using a rotary Surform rasp mounted in a drill press or similar rotating device.

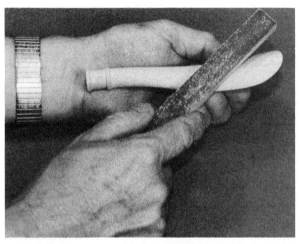

Figure 10-8h   Step 8: Sand the back of the blade to the final shape by sanding with coarse sandpaper mounted on a felt stick.

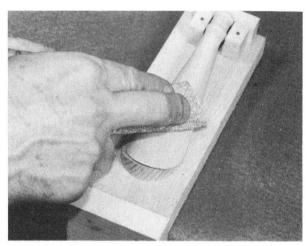

Figure 10-8i   Step 9: Fashion another holding jig to the contour of the concave side of the blade. Now sand the blade with reducing grits of paper.

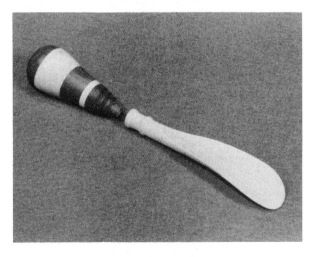

Figure 10-8j   Step 10: The handle and the blade are joined securely by drilling a $\frac{3}{8}''$ hole on the turned portion of the blade. The hole is then partially filled with epoxy cement and the handle carefully inserted until the epoxy just barely oozes out at the joint. This will ensure a complete joining of the parts and prevent any movement that might break the unit at this point.

11

Forming a carving club

While woodcarving is an individual effort, there is much to be gained through association with other carvers. Most carving clubs have had humble beginnings, usually just several people getting together once a month to enjoy a whittling session. As your little group becomes known, you will soon enjoy an increase in membership, which will create a need for organization so that you can keep it running smoothly. A larger meeting place may be needed, and you may have to look into obtaining a church hall, firehouse, community house, or school in which to hold your monthly meetings. As your group grows, so will the range of your activities, and your members will be the beneficiaries.

Organization

A well-organized club will consist of the offices of president, vice-president, secretary, and treasurer, who should each be elected annually. The president should appoint various committee chairpersons to head the following committees. (More often than not, the committee will consist of one person only, the chairman.)

Program	To arrange for outside speakers of interest to carvers and to arrange field trips.
Instruction	To set up spring and fall classes in carving-related skills.

143

Shows	To keep the club aware of carving shows held by other clubs and to provide information on guest-exhibiting.
Membership	To keep attendance and membership records.
Publicity	To publicize club activities and to arrange for showcase exhibits in libraries and banks, especially prior to the annual show. Also to maintain a club scrapbook of all newspaper publicity relating to the club and its members.
Door Prizes	To oversee and distribute door prizes at the monthly meeting.
Hospitality	To make new members welcome and to provide for refreshments at club activities.
Resources	To maintain a file of where carving-related items may be obtained.
Librarian	To oversee the club library of carving-related books.
Newsletter Editor	To write and distribute to all members the club newsletter, giving information and dates of club activities.

To keep the business portion of the club meeting to a bare minimum once it has grown in members, it is suggested that an executive committee be formed of the club officers and the committee chairpersons. This group should meet one week prior to the regular monthly meeting in order to act on all club business. The committee's findings and recommendations are then simply presented to the membership for approval. This plan greatly diminishes club business and permits the regular meeting to be devoted to carving and instruction in carving-related subjects.

Membership applications should be made up to distribute to prospective members. Also, a decision will have to be made as to annual dues to cover operating expenses.

An important part of your meetings should be a show-and-tell segment, where all carvers are encouraged to bring in some of their work and tell about it. Beginners are often reluctant to show their efforts, so understanding and special encouragement are needed in many cases. Don't be critical; rather, praise what they are doing right. Remember, we all learn from one another, and the sharing of knowledge is the paramount objective of the club.

The giving out of door prizes will spark up your meetings. The idea originated out of an effort to help keep a record of attendance. Each member upon entering the meeting place signs up for a door prize. Prizes are solicited from the members—a block of carving wood, old *Popular Mechanics* magazines, an extra tool you've had knocking about your workshop, a loaf of homemade bread or a dozen brownies. Try it; you'll keep up your attendance record and have a lot of fun besides!

A club may amount to a simple get-together of a few carvers or it may burgeon into an organization of over 150 members. The important thing to remember is that you are getting together to share the pleasure found in working with wood.

12

Carving shows and exhibiting your work

Some time ago a carver was heard to say, "Aaaaah, those carving shows, they're not for me. I carve for my own pleasure. They're for people who want their ego boosted!"

Well, we can't go along with that line of thought. Who doesn't feel a flicker of pride, to be sure, when someone in all sincerity admires a piece of their work and mentions it to them? But this carver is missing the point, because, not being professionals, we *all* carve for pleasure. Is it wrong to share the results of one's skill with others who show an interest in woodcarving?

Carving shows have much to offer. Many feature seminars in specific areas of carving—bird carving, relief work, carving in the round, and marquetry, to name a few. In addition, we are provided with the opportunity to meet and chat with carvers whom otherwise we wouldn't get to know; this also means a chance to exchange thoughts and skills. Until you exhibit at a show, you haven't experienced the fine quality of fellowship that emanates from such a gathering.

As far as trophies and ribbons go, competition is a healthy element; it spurs us on to do our very best. The monetary value of a piece of colored ribbon may be only a few cents; it is the knowledge that one's carving was chosen as a work of excellence by fellow carvers that gives that little piece of cloth a special meaning. An "ego booster"? Well, maybe in the view of some it could be so construed, but the creation of a beautiful carving is an accomplishment, and we think a person deserves to take pride in it.

Most carving clubs, as their high point of the year, hold an annual carving show. By all means, enter it. Don't be disheartened because you are a novice or because you have

Figure 12-1   Competition can spur us on to do our very best.

only a few carvings to exhibit. Pick out your best pieces, and if you feel you don't have enough carvings to exhibit, share a table with another new carver. Carving shows are a lot of fun. You will enjoy meeting and talking with other carvers and will come home with many new ideas. Enter your best piece in the competition. Who knows, you may win a ribbon in the novice class!

Setting up your display

Recently many carving shows have been awarding a prize to the carver who has the best presentation of his or her work. Plan an attractive display and shoot for it. You might think of the following list of pointers as a set of "golden rules" of carving-show exhibiting:

1. Don't display everything you've ever carved; be selective, picking out your best pieces and featuring them.

2. Through the use of tiers, create multilevels to display your small carvings at eye level. Small items should be placed high and in the back to discourage pilferage.

3. When choosing material to drape your table, stick to the plain colors; a pattern will distract from your carvings. Also, if using burlap, stay with the earthy colors—bronze, browns, dark green, natural, mustard, and so forth—which will compliment your carvings, not clash with them. The lime greens, shocking pinks, purples, bright blues, and brilliant reds are great for disco joints, but not for woodcarving shows!!

Figure 12-2   Exhibit tables.

4. Make certain your table drapes are long enough; they should come to within a few inches of the floor. This will also serve to conceal all those cartons you used to pack your carvings.

5. If you are proud of your work — and we know you are — invest a little time in a nice sign that bears your name. Use your skill to carve one; second best would be to do a neat job with those rub-on letters. Many displays are spoiled with a tacky homemade-looking sign.

6. When building your backdrop or display tiers, keep in mind that they have to be transported. It is easy to get carried away building a super backdrop only to find that it won't fit into the old family buggy or on the car-top carrier. Much is to be said for knockdown designs that can be assembled with wing-nut bolts.

7. Before a show, set up your display at home. Ask your family to be your critics and arrange carvings to their best advantage. Then take a picture of it. (If you can beg, borrow, or steal a Polaroid camera, so much the better.) Or make a sketch, marking the positions of the various carvings. You will find this a great time-saver when setting up at the show.

8. If you plan on selling, determine in advance of the show what your prices will be. Put small price tags on the pieces you want to sell, or make a list of prices for your various carvings. This way you won't be at a loss for words if someone is anxious to buy one of your items. Also make sure you have a supply of bags in which to put the sold pieces, and slip one of your carver business cards into the bag with each sale.

9. Make a checklist of everything you will need and go over it before leaving home for the show site. Don't discover when you set up your display that you have forgotten that needed extension cord or the bolts for your backdrop or that your name sign that you spent all those hours carving is back home on the wall of your workshop. Bring along pliers, hammer, screwdriver, thumbtacks, nails, cord, and some five-minute epoxy glue for emergency repairs.

149

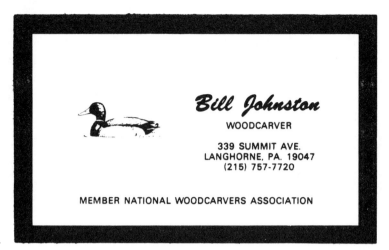

Figure 12-3   Business card.

Take along a carving that you have started and work on it during the show. Soon spectators will be crowding around to watch you work. A cheery "hello" will break the ice, and you will find you will be answering questions about carving. You should have a supply of business cards to hand out to interested people at shows and exhibits. Many card printing firms offer a selection of free logos you may use, or they will print, at no extra cost, any picture or design you furnish. You may even design your own card at no extra cost.

If you are not fortunate enough to belong to a carving club, make every attempt to enter shows anyway. The various carving magazines usually list forthcoming shows under a column entitled "Coming Events." Write to the club sponsoring the show well in advance of the show date stating that you are interested in exhibiting. You will probably receive by return mail a copy of show rules and regulations as well as an application form.

Expect to pay an entry or table fee; this money provides for the ribbons and trophy awards. If you sell, some shows expect a commission on your sales, but this will all be made clear in the show regulations.

How to ship your carvings

Should you decide to enter distant carving shows, such as the International Wood Carvers Congress in Davenport, Iowa, or the Canadian International Wood Carving exhibition in Toronto, packing your carvings will be a very important factor.

A sturdy corrugated shipping carton will be needed, or you may wish to build a crate from inexpensive plywood. Adequate cushioning material is essential if your carvings are to arrive undamaged. Styrofoam pellets or "peanuts" are excellent for this purpose. Molded empty egg cartons cut into quarters may also be utilized with satisfactory results. In a pinch, use copious amounts of crumpled newspaper.

A good method is to pack your carvings, which have been wrapped in tissue paper, in cushioning material in a carton, then pack this carton inside of a larger carton with an extra layer of cushioning between the two cartons. Tape and tie the carton securely.

You may wish to insure your shipment, which is fine for shipments within the United States. But we've learned from sad experience that the Canadian Postal Service insurance is for loss only; they will not honor any claims for damage.

Lecturing on carving

As word gets out that you are a woodcarver, the local Scoutmaster may soon be calling on you to be a guest speaker at a Scout meeting. You may be asked by the art teacher to speak to children on woodcarving. Make these commitments, if you can, for you will find there is much pleasure to be gained in talking to interested children.

Tell your young listeners that there will be a question and answer period after you have spoken. Strongly impress upon them the need for safety measures, stressing that they are not to go home and start carving unless it is under a parent's guidance. Discuss the various types of wood used and the merits of each. Bring along a variety of tools to demonstrate the uses of each. It will be of great help if you make up a set of progressive carvings of a subject; a block of wood, then a block with the side and top views drawn in pencil, then a block sawn out to form a blank, followed by a blank rounded off to the general shape, and finally the finished carving with the details carved in.

If you are talking to Scouts, band-saw out a number of simple neckerchief slide projects and hand them out to the boys for a carving project that they can work on at home. Convey the importance of sharp tools and of cutting with the grain. Explain the proper way to hold a knife and the various ways to finish the wood. At the conclusion of your talk, when all the questions have been answered, invite your listeners up to your carving exhibit table for a closer look, advising them not to touch the carvings or the sharp tools.

The rewards of exhibiting
at carving shows

At a recent carving show a survey was made of the exhibitors. Their replies to the question "Why do you exhibit at carving shows?" were as follows:

To prepare for a show, you are forced to create a new line. You are driven to excellence.

It creates a sense of individuality and self-expression. You help make others aware of their potential and of woodcarving as an art form.

It gives me the opportunity to make new friends and contacts.

It is a way to earn a little money and still have a lot of fun.

I look forward to the wonderful fellowship of friendly, caring people—almost a lost privilege in today's world.

It is a way to make extra income to expand my hobby.

I like to see the reaction of the public, to see the joy in their faces as they observe the beauty that can be created in wood.

I am proud of my work and want others to enjoy the fruits of my labor.

I like to see what other carvers are doing and get new ideas.

It is a way I can stimulate new carvers on to greater achievement; I want to share my talents.

As a selling carver, it gives me exposure. I can also travel and get to see our great country.

It is a very inexpensive training seminar.

I am a school principal, and it is a release from the pressures of my work; it gives me a new perspective.

Coming to a show and participating raises my sense of self-worth. Having been born "on the wrong side of the tracks," I note that I have now been accepted as having a special qualification. I am now in demand, I have self-respect, I am somebody.

Since I have retired, it is a great occupation. It helps keep me busy.

Simply stated, it is the best place I know just to shoot the breeze with other carvers.

Have you ever noticed the difference between the facial expressions of the people you pass on the street and those of the men, women, and children who are viewing a woodcarving show? People's faces reflect all the thoughts weighing on

152

their minds — anxiety over high food prices, the cost of gasoline, this month's electric bill, and the international situation, just to name a few. But at a woodcarving show, the signs of frustration, disappointment, worry, and open hostility seem magically to be replaced with looks of awe, wonderment, and admiration. It is great to watch the smiles break forth when viewers see the carved humorous caricatures, the looks of awe upon noticing link chains carved out of kitchen matches and toothpicks, and the many nods of appreciation at the beauty brought out of blocks of walnut by the skill and patience of a talented artist in wood.

At a carving show a few years back we had the opportunity to make an interesting study in human nature among the different exhibitors. One carver had an attractive table, with samples of his work tastefully displayed in a pleasing manner. His carvings were well done and priced at what you would pay for quality items of that nature. However, he sat behind his table with his nose in a paperback novel. So engrossed was he in his book that he seemed oblivious to the people looking at his work. As a result, the public glanced at his display and just moved on.

A second carver had about a half dozen pieces beautifully carved in walnut. The carvings were of such quality that anyone would have been proud to own one. He was overheard telling another exhibitor that he didn't carve for "the ordinary housewife," that he priced his pieces by figuring so much an hour for his time, and that he had put a price tag of $1,200 on one of them. In his opinion, which he loudly made known in no uncertain terms, any carver who painted his carvings was just covering up poor workmanship. This man, while an excellent craftsperson, spoke in such a condescending manner that he managed to repel all who approached his exhibit.

The third carver had a variety of items on his table priced from $3 to $150. He was friendly and gladly answered questions with a smile. Some of his carvings were of comic-strip characters, and he engaged in conversation about them with the children. He spoke to onlookers, asking them if they had ever tried carving, and directed them to other carvers who were selling tools and books. Clearly, he was enjoying the show to the fullest, and although he was not pushing his carvings, his sales went very well.

So there you have it — two exhibitors who went home disgruntled because the public showed little interest in their offerings, whereas the third had a great time talking with fellow exhibitors and the public as well as selling a number of his carvings. Fortunately, practically all the woodcarvers we know are like our friend who enjoys talking carving to all who view his work and looks forward to the fellowship of other carvers and renewing old acquaintances from past shows. It all seems to boil down to the fact that you can't expect the public to take an interest in your work unless you show interest in them — it's a two-way street!

Did you ever wish you had the talents of a Norman Rockwell to capture on a sketch pad or canvas all the little scenes that present themselves at woodcarving shows? Wouldn't it be great to be able to re-create that little Cub Scout as he gazes in open-mouthed awe at the whittler working on a ball in a cube surrounded by lengths of carved wooden chain of all sizes and description? And what a picture it would make to record the look of pleasure and pride on the face of a carver upon being presented with her first blue ribbon for her efforts.

Well, we can't all be Norman Rockwells, but these are some of the memories we can savor long after our carvings are packed away and our exhibit tables taken down. As one carver was heard to say, "I don't know who enjoys the carving shows more, the exhibitors or the viewing public."

How to present a successful show

In putting on a show, two factors are of prime importance: planning well in advance and having a good publicity committee. Many clubs start planning their next show nine months ahead of the projected date. Six weeks before the show the public should be made aware of your show through posters placed in schools, community houses, Laundromats, libraries, supermarkets, and other public places. Many shops will cooperate in allowing you to set up a window display to publicize your show. If you notify them in advance, newspapers will do a feature story on your carving club accompanied by photographs.

However, all these things do not come to pass overnight. Allow yourselves plenty of time and do it up right. A show coordinator should be chosen to tie together all the workings of the show committee. This committee will work out all the details of negotiating for a show site; setting the date; handling the invitations and reservations; deciding upon exhibit and competition rules; selecting the judges; and arranging for carving demonstrations, door prizes, the printing of posters and programs, newspaper publicity, and the countless details connected with the show.

Checklist for the carving show committee

The following items are those that should be given consideration by the show committee for a successful presentation.

Show site
Show date
Insurance
Security
Publicity
Reservations
Exhibiting rules
Competition rules
Judges
Admission table
Overhead banner
Judging assistants
Tables
Competition forms
Ballot counting

Registration forms
Confirmation letters
Banners
Exhibitor badges
Demonstration area
Coffee and doughnuts
Cash box
Literature table

Ribbons
Door prizes
Programs
Flyers
Scrapbook
NWCA applications
Introductory letters
Exhibit floor plan
Electrical needs
Automatic counter
Floor committee
Subscription forms
Chairs
Exhibition room measurement
Conference with manager show site
List of demonstrators
Assignment of tables
Woodcarver Show signs
Table name signs
Judging room
Ballots
Sold-item stickers
Photographer

Figure 12-4 "Anyone check with the Master Carver about giving us good weather?"

Letters to other carving clubs
Public address system
Registration acknowledgments

After the show is over, have a meeting of the show committee to review the event. Jot down things you noted that could be improved upon. You will find it invaluable when it comes to planning next year's show.

13
Random thoughts of a woodcarver

One of the authors of this book, William Johnston, is also the editor of his carving club's monthly newsletter "Chips & Quips". The following are excerpts from his column, "The Editor's Minute", which you might find amusing.

IN THE BEGINNING

God in his Heaven, in a whimsical mood,
Was struck by the beauty and luster of wood.
Said to himself, "I'll create in some way,
Someone very special, on this fine day.
I'll give him patience and knowledge to store,
And an insight to old Mother Nature's lore,
A steady hand and a sprinkling of skill
Will all be his, and much more still.
He'll be friendly and always try to be fair,
And cheerfully his talents with others will share.
He'll strive to improve, and always try harder.
By golly, I think I'll call him . . . a woodcarver!"

The helping hand

At a recent club meeting one of our members was apologizing to a fellow club member that, due to unforeseen circumstances, he had been unable to cut out a series of blanks for him as promised. It seems that a simple carving activity was planned for a project for a summer youth group being sponsored by one of the churches, and he had offered to cut out a number of blanks on his band saw for his friend.

Later on in the week the carver who was helping out with the youth group answered his doorbell to find a third club member standing on his doorstep with a big bag of sawn blanks in his arms ready for carving. It appears that this fellow had overheard the conversation at the club meeting and, without saying a word to anyone, had gone home to make them on his band saw. Whom do you think was made happier, the kids who whittled the blanks or the carver who hummed as he worked at his band saw° Kind of makes you feel good to know we have people like this in this fraternity of ours, the woodcarvers!

A master carver is our Charlie Schaal.
At shows he has quite a ball.
Says wife Alice, "Oh Lord,
Not another award,
They're already piled nine feet tall."

Recycling

Being an old Scot with heather growing out of my ears, it warms the cockles of my heart to see a carver come up with a carving of beauty made from a bit of scrap wood. Many carvers have done just that. We've seen bolo ties made out of scraps that are a joy to behold, and beautiful relief carvings have evolved from pieces of cherry that were cutoffs from a furniture-building project. Scrap rosewood from a guitar manufacturer has been transformed into attractive lapel pins and earrings. Exotic beauty lurks unseen in humble crating wood from overseas. A carver minister friend has a whole collection of carvings salvaged from church timbers from a remodeling program. Many interesting pieces of mahogany can be found in the scrap bins of local cabinetmaking shops.

It is a good feeling to see an old cedar rain gutter or lantern post transformed into a carving that can be enjoyed by all who view it for years to come. In the Chesapeake Bay area old telephone poles find themselves ending their days as carved decoys. Seems like the term *recycling* is nothing new to woodcarvers. We've been doing it for years!

Words of wisdom from an old Pennsylvania Dutch woodcarver: "Chust keep your fingers where the knife edge ain't."

158

THE CHAIN CARVER

A good old man,
He carves and whittles whenever he can.
From telephone poles to a kitchen match,
Any wood at all, onto which he can latch.
So think a while and give it some thought.
His skill is great, such patience he's got.
He'll carve a link, and then a chain.
By Golly, it's become his claim to fame.

Happiness

A few years back we were witness to a heart-warming scene at a woodcarving show. A little girl of about eight was concentrating on the small animal carvings in a glass display cabinet. Getting up her courage, she finally asked the carver about one in particular, a perfectly carved little goat about an inch high. It was a beautiful carving, the ridges on the horns, the little chin whiskers, and the cloven hooves all done to perfection. Unlocking the cabinet, the carver placed the piece in her small hand. With a look of concern on her face, a tiny wee voice asked how much it was. The carver thought a minute of the many hours he had toiled over the tiny carving, looked at her face, and said, "Oh, a dollar and a quarter."

We exchanged glances with the carver, all of us knowing full well that the carving was worth many many times over the price being asked. Eyes shining with happiness, the little girl took the quarters, dimes, and nickels out of her pocketbook and put them in the carver's hand.

Who got the better bargain—the little girl with her coveted carving or the carver who saw the happiness in the face of the child? We wonder.

Warning—woodcarver's flu

Very contagious to both sexes.

Symptoms: Continual complaint about the need for spare time, relaxation, and fresh air. Patient has a blank expression and is often inattentive to family. Can frequently be found snooping around in lumber piles, woodcarving supply houses, and catalogs. Makes secret phone calls to carving pals. Talks to self, walks with head down, constantly picking up pieces of driftwood or old cast off pieces of lumber from the ground. There is only one known cure.

159

Treatment: Victims should go immediately to the next meeting of their woodcarving club, where they will be treated to a vast array of the most beautiful woodcarvings, ideas, and good fellowship. One dose sufficient for remission; more necessary for the full cure.

A whittler rare was Lefty O'Toole
His carvings made all the girls drool.
His skill with a knife
Soon won him a wife;
Now he struggles to put eight kids through school.

Awareness

The other night I had just relit my pipe for about the fourth time, and the evening paper lay in disarray at the side of my chair, when the thought entered my old noggin, "Just what have I learned since taking up carving?" A glance at some of my early carvings and then at some of my more recent ones confirmed the fact that some improvement had been made. The lines were finer, and more detail was in evidence; the proportions were such that my birds more nearly resembled the real thing. Over the years the painting had improved, and the blending of colors seemed more natural and pleasing to the eye. Yes, I had to admit that my skills had been sharpened, and the results were gratifying.

But more than that, if my growth could be condensed into one word, it would have to be the word *awareness.* Carving has made me see things that were always there but had once escaped me. Now, looking out our back window at the birds at the feeder in the apple tree, I find myself studying their stance, the way the cock their head, their legs, and the postitioning of their feathers, and saying to myself, "When I carve my next blue jay, it's going to look just like that one." When walking in the woods or along a stream bank, my eyes just naturally seek out gnarled branches, twisted roots, and oddly shaped stones for bird mounts. Thanks to woodcarving, I am more aware of things of beauty around me. It's a good feeling!

There was a woodcarver named Hesch,
Whose work compared with the best.
Now, don't think him rude
'Cause he favors the nude;
He just likes to carve girls undressed.

Longfellow could take a worthless sheet of paper, write a poem on it, and make it worth $6,000. That is genius.

Rockefeller could sign his name to a piece of paper and make it worth millions. That is capital.

An artist can take a fifty-cent piece of canvas, paint a picture on it, and make it worth $2,000. That is art.

A woodcarver can take a scrap of wood, breathe life into it with patient hands, and make it into a priceless object of beauty. That is creativity.

OLD DAN

A carver old was Dan McNear
Who whittled and carved for many a year.
He swatted a bee when out with his wife.
Forgetting he was holding his sharp carving knife.
Now, if you listen, you will surely hear
His friends now call him, "Danny One Ear."

HAPPY HARVEY

A happy man was this fellow Harv.
He loved to whittle and he loved to carve.
He joined a club and entered the shows,
The ribbons he's won, Lord only knows.

When he passed away, 'course there was a will.
It read, "Of carving, I've not yet had my fill.
I'm not sorry to leave this old world of strife,
Just place in my hand my old carving knife.
Make sure that coffin is of straight-grained wood.
I think I know where I'm going, for I've tried to be good."

And when he got there, Saint Peter to greet,
Said, "Just give me a cloud, some wood, a few feet.
I won't take up much room, I'll be out of the way,
Happily whittling and carving, with not much to say."

Keep making chips!

Appendix: resources

Many of the following companies and individuals will furnish catalogs or descriptive literature upon request.

Publications

The CCG Log, California Carvers Guild, P. O. Box 1195, Cambria, California 93428.

Chip Chats, National Wood Carvers Association, 7424 Miami Avenue, Cincinnati, Ohio 45243.

The Mallet, National Carver's Museum, 14960 Woodcarvers Road, Monument, Colorado 80132.

National Wildlife Federation, 1412 16th Street, NW, Washington, D.C. 20036.

Wild Wings Magazine, Lake City, Minnesota 55041.

Books

H. S. ANDERSON, *How to Carve Characters in Wood*
Old West Publishing Co.
P.O. Box 990
Boulder, Colorado 80302

F. A. BRUNNER, *Manual of Woodcarving and Wood Sculpture*
F. A. Brunner
369 High Street
Westwood, Massachusetts 02090

BRUCE BURK, *Game Bird Carving*
Winchester Press
460 Park Avenue
New York, New York 10002

HAROLD L. ENLOW, *How to Carve Folk Figures and a Cigar-Store Indian* and *Carving Figure Caricatures in the Ozark Style*
Dover Publications, Inc.
31 East 2nd Street
Mineola, New York 11501

WENDELL H. GILLEY, *The Art of Bird Carving*
Hillcrest Publications
Southwest Harbor, Maine 04679

ANTHONY HILLMAN, *Carving Classic Regional Shorebirds, Carving Classic Swan and Goose Decoys, Carving Favorite Songbirds, Miniature Duck Decoys for Woodcarvers* and *Carving Early American Weathervanes*
1818 Shore Road
Seaville, New Jersey 08230

BEN HUNT, *Ben Hunt's Big Book of Whittling*
Woodcraft Supply
313 Montvale Avenue
Woburn, Massachusetts 01801

JOHN LACEY, *How to Do Wood Carving*
Woodcarvers Supply
3112 W. 28th Street
Minneapolis, Minnesota 55416

RICHARD LEMASTERS, *Wildlife In Wood*
Model Technology, Inc.
323 West Cedar
Chillicothe, Illinois 61523

ART MCKELLIPS, *Woodcarving for Beginners*
I.S.B.S., Inc.
P.O. Box 559
Forest Grove, Oregon 97116

DICK SCHNAKES, *American Folk Toys*
Mountain Craft Shop
R. 1
New Martinsville, West Virginia 26155

SHOURDS AND HILLMAN, *Carving Duck Decoys, Carving Shorebirds* and *Decorative Duck Decoys for Woodcarvers*

Harry V. Shourds	Anthony Hillman
2023 South Shore Road	1818 Shore Road
Seaville, New Jersey 08230	Seaville, New Jersey 08230

E. J. TANGERMAN, *Whittling and Woodcarving, Modern Book of Whittling and Woodcarving, Design and Figure Carving, 1,001 Designs for Whittling and Woodcarving*
The Craftshop
P.O. Box 1
Chicago Ridge, Illinois 60415

JOHN UPTON, *Woodcarver's Primer*
Garrett Wade Company
302 Fifth Avenue
New York, New York

AL VERDINI, *Comic Characters*
37 Edward Street
Worcester, Massachusetts 10605

ELMA WALTNER, *Carving Animal Caricatures*
Woodcarvers Supply
3112 W. 28th Street
Minneapolis, Minnesota 55416

Bookquick (will locate any book, in or out of print)
160 Eagle Rock Avenue, Box B
Roseland, New Jersey

GEORGE LEHMAN, *20 Realistic Game & Song Birds
Wood Carving Patterns*
624 E. Idaho
St. Paul, Minnesota 55101

Animal and bird charts

Department of Natural Resources, Tawes State Office Building, Annapolis, Maryland 21401.

National Audubon Society, 950 Third Avenue, New York, New York 10022.

Pennsylvania Game News, P.O. Box 1567, Harrisburg, Pennsylvania 17120.

Remington Arms, Inc., Bridgeport, Connecticut 06602.

Wood

Wm. Archibald, R.D. 3, Box 91A, Egg Harbor, New Jersey 08215.

John Becker, R. 2, Dyersville, Iowa 52040.

Constantine & Sons, 2950 Eastchester Road, Bronx, New York 19461.

Craftsmen's Wood Service, 2727 South Mary Street, Chicago, Illinois 60608.

Johnson Wood Products, R. 1, Strawberry Point, Iowa 52076.

Kentucky Wood Crafts, R. 1, Box 46B, Madisonville, Kentucky 42431.

Lynchburg Lumber Co. Lynchburg, Ohio.

E. J. Shiroda, 17910 Wood, Melvindale, Michigan 48122.

Woodcarver's Supply Co., 3112 W. 28th Street, Minneapolis, Minnesota 55416.

Carving blanks

Bay Country Woodcrafters, U.S. Rt. 13, Oak Hall, Virginia 23416.

Dolington Woodcrafts, Washington Crossing, Newtown Rd., R.D. 1, Newtown, Pennsylvania 18904.

Hutch Decoys, 7715 Warsaw Avenue, Glen Burnie, Maryland. 21061.

Tools

Constantine & Sons, 2950 Eastchester Road, Bronx, New York 19461.

Curtis Woodcraft Supply, 344 Grandview, Memphis, Tennessee 38111.

Power Tools & Carving Supplies, George Walker, Box 208, Chesterfield, Trenton, New Jersey 08620.

Ritter Carvers, 1559 Dillon Road, Maple Glen, Pennsylvania 19002.

Warren Tool Co., R.D. 1, Box 12B, Rhinebeck, New York 12572.

Wood Carvers Supply, 3112 W. 28th Street, Minneapolis, Minnesota 55416.

Woodcraft Supply, 313 Montvale Avenue, Woburn, Massachusetts, 01801.

Carving knives

Knott Knives, 106 S. Ford Avenue, Wilmington, Delaware 19805.

X-acto Co., 45 Van Dam Street, Long Island City, New York 11101.

Warren Tools, R.D. 1, Box 12B, Rhinebeck, New York 12572.

Sharpening stones

Russell's Arkansas Oilstones, P.O. Box 474, Fayetteville, Arkansas 72701.

H.A. Smith Whetstones, 721 Hobson Avenue, Hot Springs, Arkansas 71901.

Workbench plans

Elmer E. Jumper, 142 DiMarco Drive, Philadelphia, Pennsylvania 19154.

Branding irons

Norcrafts, P.O. Box 277, 9 Short Street, South Easton, Massachusetts 02375.

Woodcarver's Supply, 3112 W. 28th Street, Minneapolis, Minnesota 55416.

Wood stabilizers

Craftsmans Wood Service Company, 1735 West Courtland Court, Addison, Illinois 60101.

Constantines, 2050 Eastchester Road, Bronx, New York 10461.

H. E. Wheeler, 2230 East 49th Street, Tulsa, Oklahoma 74105.

Glass eyes

Elwood Supply Co., 1202 Harney, Box 3507, Omaha, Nebraska 68103.

M. J. Hofman Co., 963 Broadway, Brooklyn, New York 11221.

Tohickon Glass Eyes, Box 15, Erwinna, Pennsylvania 18920.

Van Dykes, Woonsocket, South Dakota 57385.

Jewelry supplies

Eastern Lapidary & Jewel Supply, 2218 West Chester Pike, Rt. 3, Broomall, Pennsylvania 19008.

Elwood Supply Co., 1202 Harney, Box 3507, Omaha, Nebraska 68103.

Sy Schweitzer & Co., P.O. Box 431, East Greenwich, Rhode Island, 02818.

Name badges

J. W. Spoor, 7511 N. 23rd Street, Phoenix Arizona 85020.

Index

Note: Page references in *italics* are to illustrations and patterns.

Charles Beiderman is a woodworking hobbyist and former editor of a carving club newsletter. He is now active in carving and woodcarving shows.

William Johnston has also exhibited his work in many woodcarving shows and is presently the editor of a local carving club newsletter in Pennsylvania.

Both authors have exhibited and won honors in woodcarving shows throughout the United States and Canada.